Napoleon Bonaparte

The Biography of a Leader Who Changed the History of France (Including the French Revolution)

Copyright 2018 by Adam Brown - All rights reserved.

This document provides exact and reliable information in regards to the topic and issues covered. The publication is sold with the idea that the publisher is not required to render accounting, officially permitted, or otherwise, qualified services. If advice is necessary, legal or professional, a practiced individual in the profession should be instructed.

- From a Declaration of Principles, which was accepted and approved equally by a Committee of the American Bar Association and a Committee of Publishers and Associations.

It is illegal to reproduce, duplicate, or transmit any part of this document by either electronic means or in printed format. Recording of this publication is strictly prohibited and any storage of this document is not allowed unless written permission is granted by the publisher. All rights reserved.

The information provided herein is stated to be truthful and consistent, in that any liability, in terms of inattention or otherwise, by any usage or abuse of any policies, processes, or directions contained within, is the solitary and sole responsibility of the recipient reader. Under no circumstances will any legal responsibility or blame be held by the publisher for any reparation, damages, or monetary loss due to the direct or indirect information herein.

Respective authors own all copyrights not held by the publisher.

The information herein is offered for informational purposes only, and is universal as so. The presentation of the information is without contract or any type of guarantee assurance.

The trademarks are used without consent, and the publication of the trademark is without permission or backing by the trademark owner. All trademarks and brands within this book are for clarification purposes only and are owned by the owners themselves and not affiliated with this document.

Published by Pluto King Publishing

ISBN 978-1-989711-05-7 (paperback)

Table of Contents

Introduction	**9**
Childhood and Education	**10**
The Revolution and the Rebel: 1789-1793	**27**
Formation of the First Coalition (1792 – 1797)	**43**
The Siege of Toulon (August 29 – December 19, 1793)	52
The Events of 1794 and 1795	63
Napoleon Acquires a Wife (March 8, 1796)	70
Numerous Battles with Austrians	85
Napoleon and his Italian Campaign	**105**
France's Original Intentions and Plans	109
The Battles	119
Formation of Second Coalition (December 29, 1798)	**130**
The Battles	143
Egypt after Napoleon	151
Treaty of Luneville (February 9, 1801)	163
Assassination of Tsar Paul (March 23, 1801)	167
Napoleon Treaties	172
Formation of the Third Coalition	**184**
Formation of the Fourth Coalition (October 6, 1806)	**200**
The Battles	200
Treaties of Tilsit (July 7 and July 9, 1807)	221

Treaty of Fontainebleau (October 27, 1807)	226
Battle of Medina Del Rio Seco (July 14, 1808)	238
Napoleon Enters Madrid (December 4, 1808)	247
The Wars of the Fifth Coalition	253
The Death of Napoleon Bonaparte	**285**
The Beginning of the End	287
A Revived Bonaparte	290
The Final Countdown	294
Author's Note	Error ! Bookmark not defined.

Introduction

There is no doubt that Napoleon Bonaparte has attracted legions of biographers over the last two centuries, documenting his endlessly fascinating life, associated with some of the most important and controversial events in history. A military general who became France's first emperor, Napoleon's single-minded determination for military expansion would change the world completely and revolutionize military training and organization. As such, Napoleon is considered one of the greatest military leaders the world has ever known. This biography considers this military commander whose military endeavors and sheer personality dominated Europe for over a decade. The biography throws light on this most paradoxical of men: a great military leader, an emperor and a lover.

Childhood and Education

Napoleon Buonaparte was born on August 14, 1769, in the city of Ajaccio, located on the Mediterranean island of Corsica, one year after the city had been united into the Kingdom of France. Although born in Corsica, he traveled to France at a very young age and remained devoted to his homeland throughout his life.

Napoleon's father, Carlo Buonaparte, was a lawyer who had been part of the Corsican Independence Movement, led by rebel leader Pascuale Paoli, before he eventually decided to focus on his personal life. In 1764, he married the fourteen-year-old Marie Letizia Ramolino in Ajaccio. Both families were descended from Italian mercenaries that had existed in Corsica in the beginning of the 17th century. While the Buonapartes were lawyers, the Ramolinos were a well-respected family of military people. Letizia Ramolino's father was an army officer who commanded the Ajaccio military base and held the office of inspector general of roads and bridges.

The Buonaparte family, although considered minor Corsican nobility, was not financially stable. After his marriage, Carlo was granted some of the same privileges as the upper-class French nobility. Although this didn't directly impact the family's financial status, it opened the doors of success for the younger Buonapartes, who were now allowed to attend the same educational facilities as Parisian elites.

In the 18th century, Carlo petitioned for ownership of the Mitelli estate that belonged to his brother's great-great-grandmother. The French then tried to confiscate the Mitelli estate as their asset but Carlo didn't let that happen. Legal wrangling over the matter would keep him occupied for the rest of his life, including a fight with the Ramolinos because of one of the clauses in the dowry that stated that if ever the value of property owned by Letizia fell below 7000 livres, the Ramolinos would make up the difference.

Due to this, Carlo began proceedings against Letizia's grandfather, who couldn't pay the amount even after selling most of his belongings in an auction that took place in Ajaccio's marketplace. This deeply angered Letizia as she believed in keeping up appearances. Totally offended by her husband's behavior, Letizia became vulnerable to the charms of the Comte de Marbeuf—Carlo's supporter and protector. Marbeuf believed in having male protégés on one hand and beautiful women on the other. One of his main beneficiaries was Carlo and Marbeuf turned his attention to Letizia when Carlo was away for two years in

Versailles. There's a great deal of evidence that the two were intimate while Carlo was gone.

Napoleon, the second child of eleven, showed early signs of being a liar and constantly clashed with his mother, though Carlo spoiled his kids. As a child, he was part of an extended family that included Napoleon's great uncle Lucciano, a well-known figure in Ajaccio. Lucciano played a key role in the family and his presence made a deep impact on Napoleon's life. His gifts and loans, and also the legacy he left behind for the family, helped it to cope better with poverty. However, most of the time, Napoleon was surrounded by four women—Saveria, Minama, Camilla and Geltrude. And at the center of his emotional world was his mother.

The young Napoleon was described as combative, willful and quick-witted. He certainly stood out from his siblings for his witty behavior and intellect, but he was not at all neurotic, nor did he display any megalomaniacal tendencies that might explain his later behavior. He was rather a brave and bold boy and made it very clear from early on that he wanted to become a soldier. He used to dress up like a soldier, made friends with the military troops and would even eat with them.

He started his studies at age five, in a school that was run by nuns. He was quite serious about his studies and loved mathematics. His love for the subject was seen by others when he visited a farmer's mill and calculated its production capabilities.

After getting his elementary education in Ajaccio, he was sent to the College of Autun, Burgundy, in 1779. His siblings Elisa, Lucien and Louis were still young when he left for his studies, so he barely got to know them. Caroline, Pauline and Jerome hadn't even been born at the time. Thus, Napoleon's closest sibling relationship was with his older brother, Joseph.

Seeing Napoleon's potential, the Comte de Marbeuf helped engineer a different educational arrangement. After learning about Carlo's perilous financial state, he told him how the children of French nobility could receive a free education. All parents had to do was produce their certificate of nobility and indigence. This was important as the competition was high as only six-hundred school seats were available throughout France. However, Marbeuf managed to get Napoleon a free place in a military academy and Joseph, interested in joining the church, obtained a place at Aix Seminary.

Thus, in May 1779, Napoleon was moved to the more advanced College of Brienne. The school was one of ten regional military colleges created to moderate the arrogance of young nobles but since the effort had failed, the new educational center had reverted to a school full of rich and young aristocrats, all wanting to get into the well-known École Militaire of Paris.

The military college, once a monastery, stood at the foot of a hill. Still run by monks, its aim was to prepare the children of nobility for eventual armed service. In the final year, the education was not just focused on military lessons but was rather a variant of standard training for 18th-century gentlemen. The aim was to select the best students for artillery, the navy and the engineers, and average ones for the infantry. Students who didn't perform at all well were sent back to their respective families.

Napoleon now found himself surrounded by some of the richest children in the town, who were like kings in front of him. However, he was a subsidized kid while others were paying. He felt odd, as he was in an environment that was very different from his homeland, and that was how he got the nickname "Little Corporal," since he remained buried in books of philosophy and mathematics, while his peers enjoyed lavish parties. He was also ridiculed and mocked for his Italian accent.

Napoleon's nationality, his skin, his keen desire to learn and even his name set him apart from other boys, who converted his name to "paille au nez," an insult he would never forget. He fought back but carried the scars for life. He easily accepted the

Spartan living—a tiny room, a single blanket, even during severe winters and tiresome meals. The major problem was his virulent Corsican nationalism and his belief in his father's old leader, Paoli. While other students scoffed at Paoli and believed the Corsicans were defeated, cowardly people, Napoleon always used to say that Corsicans were the bravest of the lot and this led to many fights. He also missed Joseph's company and it made him feel even more gloomy, isolated and resentful.

During 1783-84, there was heavy snowfall in the town and Napoleon, now fourteen, suggested his classmates build a fortress in the courtyard. The idea was a huge hit in the beginning, with Napoleon commanding both sides, but then things took a wrong turn when boys started covering large stones in snow, resulting in serious injuries. However, this incident was later cited as an example of his early military prowess.

At Brienne, basic Latin was the only ancient language taught. Due to this, Napoleon had to read the classical authors in translation. He did whatever it took to understand these authors and was soon recognized as one of the most able students at the school. Every year, in the months of August and September, the school used to open its doors for a kind of public exercise in which the teachers asked questions of students in the presence of state and church dignitaries. From 1780 on, Napoleon was the winner of these sessions each year. In 1781, he was awarded a prize for mathematics; in 1782, he answered questions on mathematics as well as history and in 1783, he answered mathematics questions that were as difficult as the experts could make them. Even after all this, he never got a chance to learn higher mathematics because there was no one bright enough at Brienne to teach him more advanced levels of the subject.

Though Napoleon was brilliant at mathematics, he was very poor at dancing and drawing and terrible at German. At quite a young age, Napoleon began reading the writings of Rousseau and this helped eventually transform him into both an ardent revolutionary and a brilliant commander. But this wasn't seen a positive thing at the time; he was always mocked by other French students about his dreams of achieving personal power and victory.

In 1782, the boy announced that he wanted to devote his entire life to mathematics and science, either in creating a model of the cosmos to replace the Newtonian system or in producing a general electricity theory. He decided he would join the navy and he could have been sent to either of two schools—the naval training school in Paris or the École Militaire in Paris, considered one of the best schools in Europe at the time. When it came time to make the decision, however a royal general decided that the boy had not spent enough time at Brienne. The following year, another inspector general kept the options open for Napoleon. According to him, the boy had all the right ingredients to become an excellent sailor. He was well acquainted with geography and history, well known for his mathematical applications, had excellent health and a docile expression and was weak in accomplishments.

In 1784, Napoleon earned an appointment to the École Militaire of Paris after Des Monts examined him and found him to be qualified. Here he could focus on a specific arm of the military and start learning more about the tactics. He never stopped reading and began forming his own ideas about the warfare. The program was designed for three years. However, with his outstanding work ethic and innate talent, he graduated in only a year and a half, well-prepared to take up the role of an artillery lieutenant.

In 1785, Napoleon joined the service of Louis XVI and moved on to become a lieutenant in an artillery unit at Valence. From there, he became unstoppable and the next eight years of his life can be summarized as an ascent up the ladder of French society. He started developing a strong foundation in topography and trajectory, which later resulted in his election to the Bureau of Topography for the Committee of Public Safety.

For the first time in his life, Napoleon made a true friend—Alexandre Des Mazis. Alexandre was an ardent royalist who had joined up a year ahead of Napoleon, coming from a military family in Strasbourg. He stood by Napoleon when he heard the news that Carlo Buonaparte had died and his family was left in financial limbo. Napoleon wrote to his Uncle Lucien, asking him to take care of the family until he became an officer. Though the death of the father created sudden financial anxiety in Napoleon's life, the sorrow didn't last long. He scorned Carlo when he couldn't see any great or remarkable achievements to his credit. His feelings for his father completely changed and this could be clearly seen in his actions. He rejected Montpellier Municipal's proposal of constructing a monument in Carlo's remembrance, stating: "Forget it! Let's not trouble the peace of the dead. Leave their ashes in peace. I also lost my grandfather, my great grandfather, why is nothing done for them?"

Later, Napoleon told everyone that his father's death was a happy one as he would have made political blunders that would have finished Napoleon's career before it even had a chance to get started. But even after all this, he sought a father figure and found one in Paoli.

There were two stages that were required as part of admission into the elite French officer corps—first was the examination on the artilleryman's bible, followed by a year in artillery school. After this, the second stage was comprised of testing students on Bezout. All those who could clear this two-stage process were commissioned as second lieutenants. Only a very few outstanding students could take all four volumes in one examination and gain straight admission into the regiment. Napoleon was one of those elite, finishing his exams in one go in 1785.

Every year, an eminent personality used to come to the military school to test the knowledge of the artillery school students and in 1785, it was Pierre Simon, Marquis de Laplace—a well-known scientific genius of the 18th century. He was a great mathematician, specialized in astronomy, whose theories could be used to explain the motion of Jupiter and Saturn and its moons, electromagnetic physics, the nebulae in the deep space and so on. He put Napoleon to a rigorous test comprised of algebra and differential equations as well as mathematical applications. In all the schools and colleges of France, there were only 58 students studying to take on an artillery position, and among these Napoleon was the forty-second person. Being forty-second out of 58 created a notion that Napoleon was not that bright even though he was better than students who had had two years of additional study. Considering all these factors and looking at his dedication, he was commissioned as a second lieutenant. Although he really deserved it, some speculated this was an ulterior move as the La Fere regiment was known to have served Corsica for years.

Napoleon was not prepared to live a military life when he entered the army. He was more of an 18th-century gentleman, equipped with a classical education; he was yet to learn the skills of a real soldier on the battlefield. If the schools in Paris and Brienne were designed to promote equality on social grounds, as they claimed, they failed in the case of Napoleon. The experience of being a poor student among filthy rich cadets left him cynical. The bullying he endured for being a poor Corsican made him grow to hate aristocrats. Napoleon hated them so much that he referred to them as a curse upon the nation, and this hatred became even worse after seeing the aristocratic disrespect for minorities, however talented they might be. But Napoleon was lucky enough to get into artillery, the only branch of the army where talent was genuinely appreciated.

By the time he left Brienne, he had lost his religious faith because of three major reasons. First, he had experienced force feeding of rote doctrine at Brienne, by monks. Second, he had read Rousseau, who emphasized civil religion being the ideology of the state and hated Catholicism for acting as a bridge between the citizen and society. Lastly, the monks at Brienne taught their students that classical authors were being roasted in hell because they were pagans, which angered the boy who was so intrigued by the ancient world. Napoleon became a pessimist and stopped believing in redemption in any form.

Napoleon also always faced difficulties in making friends, and the ones he did make often let him down. He was cheated by Fauvelet de Bourrienne, who painted an idyllic picture of the two bathing in Aube's icy cold waters. Bourrienne's army career was spoiled but Napoleon helped him by appointing him as his secretary. It turned out Bourrienne was a money launderer—a fraudster who cheated Napoleon at every opportunity.

In 1785, when he visited Madame Permon, an old Corsican friend of Carlo's who had married a rich French commissary office, Napoleon met her two daughters, Laure and Cecile. Due to the instant antagonism that arose between Laure and Napoleon, she called him "Puss in Boots." He didn't like her at all, though she later married Junot, one of Napoleon's friends. She was the female version of

Bourrienne as she would also do anything for money. With the personal baggage of his nationality and social origins, bad experiences with male friends and fear of women, Napoleon really found it difficult to trust the human race.

In 1785, Napoleon left the École Royale Militaire, Paris, and before joining the La Fere regiment, he decided to see his patron, Marbeuf, who used to stay at Abbey Palace. He stayed there for two days and then completely his journey to Valence. The La Fere regiment was known for its tough life—rise early, work hard and give your best till you dropped. Buonaparte was at number four in the bombardier companies. He had to undergo ten weeks of rigorous training comprised of basic training and drilling as a private and then as a sergeant. Finally, in January 1786, he completed his probationary period as an officer, during which he led a not-so-tough life as a mounting guard, attending classes on various subjects, looking after the men, rock climbing, skating, traveling etc.

The major problem he faced during those days was money. Although he earned a decent amount, most of his earnings went toward paying off his impoverished family's debts back in Corsica. All this forced him to manage with just the basics—he found basic lodging and ate in cheap cafés.

At this point, Napoleon decided to launch himself as a writer. He wrote a book about an Arab prophet who was defeated and therefore committed suicide along with his followers. This book was the outcome of his fascination with the life in Middle East and his pessimism about the cruel world he lived in. He once wrote, "Always alone in the midst of men, I return to dream with myself and give myself up to all the force of my melancholy. What madness makes me desire my own destruction? Without doubt, the problem of what to do in this world. Life is a burden to me because I feel no pleasure and because everything is affliction to me. It is a burden to me because the men with whom I have to live, and will probably always live, have ways as different as mine as the light of the moon from that of the sun. I cannot then pursue the only manner of living that could enable me to put up with existence, whence follows a disgust for everything."

The uneventful phase of life at Valence finally came to an end in 1786 when the regiment was asked to suppress a strike by silk workers. Napoleon then expressed his homesickness and applied for leave so that he could visit his folks back in Corsica. After being away from the island for almost eight years, he finally reached home in September 1786. Although clouded by dark financial shadows, the reunion with family was quite a joyous one for Napoleon. There, he discovered a change in the political climate. Agents of Paoli, backed by English gold and direction from Tuscany by Clement—Paoli's brother—were propagandizing in the hinterlands of Corsica, which was off limits to French soldiers and officials. Although he didn't involve himself in all this, he didn't hesitate to express his desire to make Corsica independent.

Napoleon's mother was so occupied with domestic issues and money matters that she couldn't see her son's infatuation with the French Enlightenment in the form of Rousseau's writings or his fulminations against dictatorial France. Even his Uncle Lucien, who was guarding gold stashed under his bed, didn't seem to be a helpful companion for a rebellious young Corsican. As usual, Napoleon didn't expect anyone to support him; he liked his own company. Many a time he used to ride alone in the countryside, drinking the clear water from lovely mountain streams and breathing in fresh air with a refreshing fragrance of orange blossoms.

In April 1787, he wrote to his commanding officer, attaching a medical certificate proving that he was ill and asking to extend his stay in Corsica. His request for an extension of leave was granted on health grounds and he was told that he didn't need to report back to work until December 1787. He made the most out of it by visiting different places, such as theaters (opera being his favorite pastime).

Napoleon then made yet another request for an extension of leave, for another six months. This time the reason he gave his officer for the extension was that he wanted to attend a Corsican meeting. As he asked them not to pay him for his absence, his leave was granted.

By 1788, the financial condition of the family had become worse as Letizia had four kids who were entirely dependent on her for everything. Napoleon decided to leave Ajaccio in June 1788 after he got a chance to see his brother Joseph, returned from Pisa with a title of doctor of laws.

By now, the La Fere regiment had been stationed in Auxonne and Napoleon took lodgings at the Pavilion de la Villa, which was near the barracks. He had just two friends in the barracks—Des Mazis and Captain Gassendi, a distinguished geometer, man of letters and an admirer of Corsica. There was nothing much to do in Auxonne, and even for the parade, he was required to appear just a week. This was when he decided to utilize all his free time in writing and reading different pieces. He also got into a habit of rising by 4:00 a.m., having just one meal at 3:00 p.m., to save money, and going back to sleep at 10:00 p.m., after spending eighteen hours with his books. This ascetic way of living affected his health badly—the poor, insufficient diet, living in a cold and damp climate, overwork and lack of sleep triggered physical exhaustion and his body fell prey to malaria.

Napoleon's mathematical skills impressed a mathematics instructor, Professor Lombard, who mentioned him in front of all troops in Auxonne as "one to note." The Corsican had unmatched knowledge of ballistics and projectiles and also spared some time to hone his skills as a draughtsman. He was greatly influenced by a general's brother whose handbook talked about the massing of big guns in battle. He was also influenced by Jacques de Guibert, whose books described a successful army's dependence on speed. The influence of all these writers was so much that Napoleon filled thirty-six manuscript books in fifteen months, with writings on history, philosophy and artillery. He also became the second lieutenant to take over the position of a select artillery committee. The only thing in the way of his promotion was his uncertain health. He suffered from another attack of fever, after which he wrote to his mother about his ill health.

The Revolution and the Rebel: 1789-1793

In the spring and summer of 1789, events in France moved really fast. King Louis XVI called a meeting comprised of representatives from the First Estate, the clergy; the Second Estate, nobility and the Third Estate, commoners, to discuss the matters of taxes. The impasse came to an end in June when the commoners declared themselves as the sole representatives of the country and called for a national assembly. This was followed by another meeting where the king instructed them to confine the discussion to tax matters. However, Louis wasn't strong enough to salvage the situation by making minor compromises.

In early October, Versailles Palace was attacked by armed bands who forced their way into the assembly and pushed into the palace. They killed the guards and finally managed to reach the king. Looking at the situation, Louis agreed to move the royal residence to Paris. A few days after the fall of Bastille, a riot broke out when a rebel mob sacked the tax office. After a couple of months, a group of soldiers forced the regiment to give them the slush funds that had been designed for their welfare. This was the last straw for Napoleon, who had recently taken the oath prescribed by the Constituent Assembly. He realized that an agitated army without discipline was nothing more than an armed mob that could prove to be dangerous to anyone who confronted it. On the other hand, he knew that Corsica needed him.

Conflicted, Napoleon learned that the Paoli party wanted to gain independence from France. If this was true, the Corsican guard could play an important role. He once again decided to apply for leave, realizing that his country and family should be more important for him at the moment. His leave was granted and he sent instructions to his uncle to start preparing the ground for his rebellious plan in Corsica.

In late September he arrived in Ajaccio and found his family in terrible financial straits. Laws, taxes, regulations—nothing had changed and the old people of Corsica continued to run the island, subsidized and protected by the French. Apart from the royalists, there were two political movements that existed during that time—the young liberals and the Paolists led by Paoli from London. Paoli was pushing for the French in London to make Corsica a free French territory which he could then rule as a dictator.

Backed by Joseph, who had returned from Italy after studying law, Napoleon threw himself into the Paolist movement, whose ultimate goal was to seize the French fort that stood tall in Ajaccio and force the French people to depart from their land. For this to happen, it was important to replace the French committee with a rebel committee. In no time, Napoleon added one more goal to the mission—creating an island-wide armed military, thus freeing the land from the French. The French assembly received a formal petition requesting these changes and then passed it on to the Committee of Twelve to approve it. But the petition was rejected by the committee, igniting rebel protests. This led to anarchy and Napoleon wanted to seize the citadel and chase them from the island. But the rage and threat were countered by a Swiss regiment from Corte and French commissaires who dissolved the national guard.

Seeing all this, Napoleon wrote a letter to the National Assembly—a protest letter that refuted every objection to the island military suggested by the Committee of Twelve. This letter of protest was sent to several French people and proved to be quite remarkable. It could have led to a death sentence for treason by a French officer.

Even though there were political issues and confusion in the country, its assembly and government had their own reasons for the issues around Corsica. Some of the local uprisings led the French to believe that the bandits and savages in Corsica would never submit and that was why they withdrew their forces from the island. But this was not agreed upon by the royalist delegate Buttafuoco, who advised the French people to make Corsicans obey them, referring to them as "shabby people who deceive themselves with grand words and in reality lack the courage to fight for their objectives."

However, the French assembly was not really okay with this punitive action. With his fellow delegates, Saliceti, a dissenter, wanted Corsica to become an integral part of France so that the newly integrated nation guaranteed an opportunity for Corsicans to build their future in France. He also wanted them to return to their homes. Later, two powerful assembly leaders, Volney and Mirabeau, demanded approval for integrating Corsica, which was agreed upon by the legislators. Although Paoli's proposal was never submitted to the assembly, the general wrote a flattering letter showing his excitement over Corsica becoming an integral part of the French nation. The punitive expedition into Corsica was canceled and certain restraints were enforced on the interference of army in Corsica's matters. All this surprised Napoleon as the assembly had shown neither a wish for a Corsican national guard nor for a central committee.

In 1790, rumors about the French government abandoning the island, contrary to the assembly decree, disturbed Corsicans. Due to this, there were several major outbreaks between the French government and the locals, and conditions didn't improve even when Paoli arrived in Paris. This was not the time for Napoleon to leave his home island, and, realizing this, he audaciously asked for an extension of his leave. His leave was granted and he continued his plan of taking control of the French fortress and turning the city into a revolutionary community.

However, instead of becoming the master of Corsica by striking a deal with Paoli, Napoleon found himself to be a pariah. To add to this, Paoli enjoyed taking over his mission of reorganizing what had turned into a department of France. He executed and succeeded in his mission and became the president of the elected directorate. And the pariah, on the other side, was suspected of plotting and was no longer able to walk on the city streets without somebody to escort him. Looking at him, the crowd used to scream, "Death to the officer. Death to the Jacobins." He was once even cornered by a raging group of penitents and was rescued with a lot of difficulty.

Due to his candor, Napoleon's eventual meeting with Paoli was also a disaster. In an incident when the general was explaining his defeat by the French, he commented that it was Paoli's deployment of troops that had made the defeat unavoidable.

Despite all of this and his perilous existence in Corsica, Napoleon decided to remain an active member of the Jacobin club. This not only made him overstay his leave but also led him to ignore the order that commanded all officers to return to their respective regiments.

The delinquent young Corsican lingered on for another month until it was confirmed that the French would not let Corsica form its own national guard. He then left for France in February 1791, with his brother Louis.

Napoleon returned to France, a country that was breaking into pieces and the power of which was in the hands of certain leaders who wanted to turn it into an autocratic state which could then be governed by them. These delegates, also known as "Legistes," were common people; most of them belonged to a family of lawyers who had served the royalty for years. But now they had just one mission, one idea—to transfer all the powers from the royal throne to the commoners, although they were opposed by various religious members, nobles and middle-class people. The middle-class people wanted to at least put a check on the powers of the government, something similar to America's Constitution. But there were issues. Many people in the provinces had an interest in a constitutional monarchy, and not just the deputies. These were people who had lived without feudal privileges and various other benefits, but they wanted the monarchy to continue, despite the failure of the royal powers. This was a strange situation as the powerful Legistes had gotten rid of the traditional governing bodies by bringing in a system of self-directed municipal directorates, each functioning independently and not in favor of each other. This resulted in anarchy and the assembly deployed empowered representatives to deal with it.

Napoleon's ambitious plan couldn't take off. The president of the department of Corsica, Paoli had turned into a powerful dictator, especially with his old cronies that saw the French Revolution as an effective way to gain independence for Corsica. By this time, Napoleon was being supported by his Uncle Lucien, who was on his deathbed, and his legacy eased the financial issues of the Buonaparte family. Napoleon still hoped for getting the command of the national guard but when it became clear that Paoli was not going to offer him anything, Napoleon, along with his Jacobin friends, organized elections for deputy lieutenant colonel of the Ajaccian volunteer battalion. As Lieutenant Colonel Quenza, Napoleon's senior, didn't have any experience in military, command was virtually taken over by Napoleon. His career aspirations had shifted to Corsica and he wanted to force Paoli to offer him top command in the guard. But when his leave expired in December, all his thoughts and plans sank and he didn't sail for France.

Napoleon just didn't want to give up and he persuaded his commanding officer that their troop must replace the French guard in the fortress that he was targeting. His idea was totally rejected by Paoli and that was when he convinced Quenza to attack the citadel in April that year. After numerous deaths and a fight that lasted for three days, French supporters decided to put an end to it and this left Napoleon as a pariah again. The incident was reported to the French ministry, where Napoleon was already not in the good books.

In 1792, Napoleon arrived in France at a very crucial time when the government, the army, the assembly, the revolution and the people had reached an important milestone. Although the new assembly was the main player, the Legistes still had the preponderant voice over key issues and matters. But the new deputies were mostly young people who had different views on preserving the monarchy versus transitioning into a revolutionary state. This bunch of young lawyers soon found themselves becoming slaves to their own revolutionary act but things took a complete turn when Austria and Prussia threatened invasion.

In 1793, Napoleon returned to Corsica even though he knew he was out of favor with Paoli and that

Paoli was suspected by the Jacobins of wanting to raise an independent Corsica that could then be swallowed by England. Additionally, he knew the island was being ruled by Paoli, who now had Borgo (Buonaparte's enemy) as his executive agent. So what was his reason for suddenly returning home? Was it that he considered himself an orphan who would be set loose in the French nation when the revolution ended? Or was it the call of his home island and family, combined with the desire to take revenge on his enemies? None of these reasons really answer why he ardently believed in the French Revolution. Something must have happened in France that provoked him to behave this way. Did Saliceti, who had become an important voice in the assembly, send Napoleon back to Corsica to spy on Paoli's activities? Did he promise him a favor if he would report Paoli's activities and serve as an agent?

When back in Corsica, Napoleon behaved as if he was sponsored by some powerful body. He reestablished himself in the Ajaccio battalion as deputy commander in the rank of lieutenant colonel. The closeness between Saliceti and Napoleon could be clearly seen by the long letters he wrote to the young captain, complaining of the Paoli regime's attempts to put the island on the defensive, particularly at this crucial time when France was on the eve of maritime war. Just after the execution of the royal king and queen, Napoleon wrote a letter to the French ambassador stating that, "the Convention has without doubt committed a great crime and I deplore it more than anyone; but, come what may, Corsica should always be united to France. This is the only way Corsica can exist. My friends and I, I assure you, will defend the cause of this union."

Napoleon was instructed by the war minister to suggest the most suitable defense of the island—this certainly influenced his tactical thinking. After discussing things with his peers, Napoleon mentioned that it would not be possible to secure the entire island's gulf and bays. Therefore, the next point was to identify the most important gulf and fortify it. Napoleon identified St. Florent after surmising that its harbor could hold a large fleet and measuring its proximity from France. He then submitted his ideas for its fortification after personally analyzing its surroundings. He also suggested that Ajaccio should be defended with artillery batteries by the harbors. His suggestions were sent to Paoli, who believed that the island's defense was not anybody's concern, at least not France's.

As Napoleon had thought, Paoli was ordered by the French minister to take an expeditionary force to seize Sardinia. Paoli was unhappy as he considered it a natural ally of his island and Sardinia's king had always been friendly with Corsica. Even so, they invaded the rich states of Savoy and Nice to end the rule of King Victor. Colonel Colonna Cesari, Paoli's nephew, ordered the Corsican battalion to seize Maddalena Island to use it as a base for further movement. Napoleon was elated. Paoli had always been his hero and inspiration. But his return as a "brat without experience" displeased Paoli so much that he asked Colonel Colonna to have nothing to do with Napoleon. Initially, Paoli tried controlling the situation with words, but eventually he ordered Colonna to do whatever it took to ruin Napoleon's expedition.

In February that year, the not-so-well equipped Ajaccio battalion sailed and seized a small portion of the target island and arranged a setup for opening fire on the neighboring fortified island. But then Colonna, apparently faced by the threat of a mutiny, canceled the operation and ordered the Corsican battalion to go back home. Although Napoleon didn't agree to this decision, he was forced to give in and throw his cannons into the water. Although this was a great achievement for Paoli, Napoleon started treating him not only as a disloyal enemy of France but also a personal enemy.

All this while, Napoleon was supporting the Ajaccian Jacobins. However, he was a supporter of

Bartolomeo's vendetta against the general and sent a note regarding the failure of expedition. Copies of this strongly-worded note were even sent to the French war minister, the commanding general of the Army of the Alps and Saliceti. All of this severely damaged Paoli's reputation in the eyes of the French people. A famous author of the time, Constantin Volney, had harsh words published in a French newspaper. Paoli further provoked problems when he refused to make the trip due to his advancing age.

Saliceti, along with two commissaries, was asked to visit the island to look into the matter of allegations again the old Brit and that was when they arrived in Bastia in April. This resulted in an undeclared war and the commissaries declared Paoli's financial acts as slanderous to the French superiors. Looking at the whole scene, Paoli moved to Corte, taking all the treasury with him. This left the commissaries with an angry island. Saliceti also decided to visit Corte to get Paoli to come back to Bastia but, upon being refused, he returned to Bastia alone. From there, he again wrote to Paoli, who learned that the convention had ordered his arrest.

While all this was happening, Napoleon was busy preparing for the Sardinian expedition while his brother Lucien, now eighteen, had befriended the Marquis de Semonville, the newly appointed French ambassador to Corsica. Semonville wanted to address the Jacobin club but since he didn't know the language, he requested Lucien interpret for him. He was so impressed by the young Corsican that he hired him as the secretary of his embassy. They couldn't reach Turkey, due to the British blockade, so they had to return to France. All the while, Lucien continued to be a Jacobin and a speaker at their club.

While all this was happening, Napoleon had been named an inspector of artillery by the commissaries and he wasn't aware of the dangers that surrounded him and his family. An improvised assembly, led by Paoli, sentenced the Buonapartes to shame and insult, which meant a death sentence in Corsica. A well-wisher suggested Napoleon leave the city before he was caught and assassinated, which he did. This was followed by several days of arrest and escape, after which he decided to join the commissioners. The island was in complete insurrection but Letizia somehow managed to get her family to the coast, where they were rescued by Napoleon and boarded a ship to France.

The French Revolution took a melodramatic turn in February 1793 when the revolutionaries turned the tables on the Austrians and Prussians. By the end of 1792, the new armies had invaded the Austrian Netherlands and the Rhineland, spreading the ideology of the revolution. At the beginning of 1793, Louis XVI was executed and a new doctrine for France's natural frontiers—the Alps, the sea, the Rhine and the Pyrenees—was announced. Keeping the aspirations of the nation in mind, war was declared on two countries—Spain and England. An expedition against Sardinia, which held strategic importance in the Mediterranean, was a sign of new policies by expansionists. The invasion demonstrated France's newfound powers.

With a flotilla of ships and a large body of regulars, Admiral Truguet arrived in Ajaccio with the intention of incorporating the Corsican volunteer battalion into his armed force. There were clashes between sailors and soldiers, and on top of this there were now issues between regulars and Corsican volunteers. This venture was opposed by Paoli, who was now close to Revolutionary France, but he was smart enough to see that Truguet's regulars might join Napoleon's volunteers to overthrow him if he opposed the venture openly. There were high chances of this, especially because there were rumors that Truguet was quite close to the Buonaparte family. Looking at the situation, Paoli therefore secretly schemed to rid Ajaccio of Napoleon's volunteers and ensure the failure of Truguet's project.

Looking at the clashes between volunteers and regulars, Paoli swayed Truguet into two attacks—at Cagliari and a diversionary thrust against La Maddalena, one of the largest Buccinari islands, located between Corsica and Sardinia. For the second attack on La Maddalena, along with its two forts, Paoli made his nephew Cesari colonel, along with Napoleon. But the signs of the venture didn't seem to be great from the very beginning. Gales of wind forced the ships back to Ajaccio. A surprise attack was planned for the night but Cesari ruled it out. Even today, no one knows the exact series of events that occurred. It is believed that the sailors appeared to force Cesari to call off the entire project but Napoleon and various other analysts believed that there was no such mutiny at all and it was all a part of preplanned strategy between Paoli and his nephew.

La Maddalena was a disaster and Napoleon was really furious. He felt betrayed and decided to sever all bonds with Paoli for good. He requested an interview with the man he had once worshipped, which turned into a heated confrontation. Napoleon started on a friendly note, considering the fact that if a civil war happened, the Paoli followers were going to win. He requested Paoli not turn away from the venture that had been founded on the interests of the nation, but Paoli replied angrily, mentioning how things had gone sour and how France's leaders wanted a submissive Corsica, and not the independent one that Napoleon had been fighting for. Paoli stormed from the room and the two men never saw each other again after that moment.

With his pride injured, Napoleon needed time to heal his wounds and take stock. He started feeling that all he had done to save his land was not worth it and it had all been a big mistake. He felt like giving up on everything and moving to a place where he could live in peace—away from the work, away from the home island for which he had done all this.

Formation of the First Coalition (1792 – 1797)

The absolutist regime that had been ruling France for so many years was almost at its end by 1791. An informal National Assembly (a revolutionary assembly, comprised of the common people), which had been formed in 1789, was in power. It continued to exert its authority over the presiding monarch at that time, King Louis XVI. He was not happy at being a constitutional monarch. Therefore, he tried to escape to Varennes in June 1791. However, the revolutionaries managed to capture him and placed him under house arrest. Some members of the king's court secretly hoped to receive help from other nations in restoring the throne to the deposed king. However, for months, European states refused to help, facing problems of their own. The Ottoman Empire, Austria, Russia and Prussia were jostling amongst themselves for superiority in Eastern Europe. Things changed when Poland, stuck in the middle of these power struggles, decided to create a new constitution. In actuality, Poland was only following the same path that France had taken, but it sufficed to jolt Austria into thinking that it had to initiate some kind of an alliance which would prevent the eastern rivals from fighting amongst themselves, and instead, help in restoring the monarchy in France.

Towards this end, on August 27, 1791, Leopold II and King Frederick William II came together to issue the Declaration of Pillnitz. Renowned as the Holy Roman Emperor, Leopold II was the king of Bohemia and Hungary from 1790 to 1792. He was also the Archduke of Austria, as well as the Grand Duke of Tuscany from 1765 to 1790. King Frederick William II was the sovereign of Prussia. These two rulers were immensely worried that the French Revolution would inspire other nations to begin their own revolutions. They were also under great pressure from French émigrés, that is, the people who had run away from France. These émigrés wanted King Louis XVI back on the throne. The king's wife, Marie Antoinette, was the sister of Leopold II. He was worried about her safety. Therefore, the two rulers met at Saxony, in Germany, and created a five-sentence declaration, urging all sovereign rulers in Europe to view the situation in which the King of France found himself as a matter of great concern. It was imperative that all of them come together in order to restore monarchical governance in France. At the same time, the two rulers took care to keep the wording ambiguous enough that no one would think of declaring war against France. They hoped that it would provoke the revolutionaries to adopt conciliatory procedures, as well as appease the French émigrés.

Unfortunately, the émigrés and the revolutionaries did not take the declaration lightly or happily! The former strove to gain support from foreign armies, while the latter's National Assembly declared war on Austria on April 20, 1792. In retaliation, Austria and Prussia came together to form an alliance titled the First Coalition. Later on, Great Britain, The Netherlands, Sardinia and several other Italian States, Spain and Russia joined them. The coalition lasted from June 26, 1792 right through October 1797. This was the longest-lasting coalition among the seven coalitions that would ultimately exist. It was also the stepping stone for Napoleon Buonaparte to catapult himself into the limelight and remain there until 1814.

Although Napoleon himself did not take part in the attack directly, he was in Paris at the time of the siege. Additionally, witnessing these events paved the way for his own rebellion and capture of the throne of France.

At the time of the siege, King Louis XVI and his family were residents at the Tuileries Palace, a dilapidated castle located on the banks of the Seine River, vastly different from the grandeur of the Versailles Palace. Even the Legislative Assembly conducted its affairs at the Tuileries. The king's house arrest did nothing to improve matters. France's economic condition continued to deteriorate, and the citizens always remained in fear of foreign invasions. After all, the majority of the world had sympathy for King Louis XVI and his sufferings! It did not help that the Duke of Brunswick, Karl Wilhelm Ferdinand, (Field Marshal of Prussia) added fuel to the fire by declaring that he would wreak vengeance on the people of France if they dared to harm the king or his family. This war manifesto on July 25, 1792, prompted journalists to incite the people further against the Royal Family and their supporters. With the help of Maximilien Robespierre (leader of the violent Jacobin Revolutionaries) and Georges Danton (a powerful orator), the people decided that they would attack the king's new residence on August 10.

That morning, a huge crowd, comprised of thousands of people, gathered outside the Tuileries Palace. People carried pikes, guns, scythes, sabers, iron bars, sharp pieces of wood and daggers. Deciding that he did not want to slaughter his own people, the king and his family moved to the Legislative Assembly building. He did not have the support of the National Guard or the gendarmes handy, for the majority had fled Paris the previous night, fearing for their own lives. Therefore, only the Swiss Guard remained in charge of a fortress-like building which was strong and solid enough to protect all the people hiding within it. To make a long story short, the mob breached the gates quickly and entered the courtyard to begin a horrifying massacre. Palace staff, members of the Swiss Guard and courtiers were beheaded, as well as stripped of their belongings and clothes. The crowd even fed dismembered body parts to dogs. By midday, just 250 members of the Swiss Guard had lived to tell the tale. The mob decided to throw them into prison. The same crowd would kill all of them, four weeks later, in September.

At midday, the mob surrounded the Legislative Assembly building. People demanded the abolition of the monarchy and the dissolution of the Legislative Assembly. Outnumbered, the assembly's deputies acquiesced. They would suspend the king and put a five-man executive council in place, as a replacement. Furthermore, there would be democratic elections in September, for the initiation of a new national convention. Following this announcement, King Louis XVI and his family were imprisoned in the Square du Temple's tower in northern Paris. People abandoned the Constitution of 1791 too. With the abolition of all feudal dues, the revolutionaries even put an end to seigneurialism. When the Marquis de Lafayette strove to organize a counter-revolution for restoring the monarchy, the people turned against him, forcing him to flee France. Later, the Austrians took him prisoner.

The next significant event to take place that year was the Battle of Valmy. There was nothing significant about Napoleon being part of this battle, for he continued as an ardent revolutionary in the French Army, and nothing more. The battle itself, however, proved significant as the newly- formed French Republic managed to stand on its own feet and saved itself from early destruction. This was despite the confidence that the Austrians and Prussians had about overcoming the French Army easily. This confidence stemmed from the fact that earlier on, a French attack upon the Austrian Netherlands (modern Belgium) had ended in disaster. Instead of setting the Austrian Netherlands and Austria against one another as the French Army had hoped, it found itself on the run instead! The fault lay with the French Foreign Minister at that time, Charles Dumouriez, who had believed that turning one army against another would help to keep France safe against its enemies.

Nonetheless, this time around, the scenario was different. The Allied forces had an impressive army, comprised of 8,000 to 15,000 French émigrés; 40,000 to 42,000 Prussians; 29,000 to 30,000 Austrians and around 5,000 Hessians. The forces were highly enthusiastic but lacked unity thanks to the presence of two egotistic leaders. One was the Duke of Brunswick, who felt that they should set up a strong base on the borders of France, such that a future invasion would prove easier to handle. The other was the Sovereign of Prussia, who decided that a stronger policy was necessary. Finally, they agreed to opt for a direct invasion, capture some fortresses along the way and overrun Paris. With regard to the French Army, it was comprised of the Armée du Nord (north), the Armée du Centre (center) on the eastern side and the highly experienced Royal Artillery at Valmy.

In the beginning, the progress of the Allied forces was slow, but steady. They managed to reach Valmy without too much trouble on September 20. The French Army was waiting for them, having positioned itself on the hills around Valmy. Divided into two units, the army was almost 55,000 strong. When the two armies came face to face with one another, the Allied forces had their backs towards Paris, while facing east. The French Army stood between these forces and Germany while facing west.

Although the war continued for the next ten days, neither side suffered heavy casualties. The Duke of Brunswick did feel impressed by the French Army's ability to stand up to its opponents' heavy artillery fire, without flinching. The French attitude made him quite unwilling to launch a full-scale attack on France. Additionally, during that time, political developments inside France ensured that it became a republic. Therefore, King Frederick William II decided that it would be best to negotiate for peace. However, he also demanded a return to monarchical rule. The French replied that they would negotiate only when all the Prussians had vacated French territory. Unsurprisingly, the negotiations fell through. The Allied forces decided to leave France and go back. The retreat lasted until October 23, 1792, since the forces took some time to move through France and go beyond its boundaries. Thus, the French Revolution continued, despite the imprisonment of the king.

The victory only served to increase Minister Dumouriez's thirst for war! He decided that the way was clear for attacking the Austrian Netherlands. This time around, he was also in charge of the Armée du Nord on the battlefield. Furthermore, he had able generals to assist him, along with an advantage in numbers. To illustrate, the French Army was comprised of 13 battalions of volunteers, 32,000 infantry, 4,000 soldiers, 115 guns and 3,800 cavalrymen. It helped that plenty of experienced men were in the army, which would prove of great help in outflanking the weaker sections of the Austrian Army. As for the Austrians themselves, their army was comprised of over 20,000 soldiers, 11,600 infantry, fifty-six guns and 2,170 cavalrymen. The person in charge was the governor of the Austrian Netherlands. If this was not all, there were three other generals, who had sufficient infantry and cavalry each to ensure a sure defeat of the French Army. Nonetheless, France's artillery bombardment set the tone for the battle that followed.

Dumouriez's tactics worked very well, forcing the Austrians to retreat. By the time the battle ended, France had suffered 2,000 casualties, while the Austrians had suffered only 828. Regardless, France took over the Austrian Netherlands. They moved towards Brussels, finally occupying the city on November 14, 1792. Although France could hold onto the Austrian Netherlands for a short time only, it used this time to its advantage. The revolutionaries worked on instilling new ideas about liberty and freedom into the minds of a generally conservative populace. Although Dumouriez was not able to enjoy his triumphs for long, he did ensure that the French Republic remained militarily stable.

The next year was an eventful one, beginning with the execution of King Louis XVI. The Revolutionaries sent him to the guillotine on January 21, 1793. This increased the fervor of other European nations to bring France to its knees. As a result, the France was united under an umbrella of nationalism.

The Austrians decided that it was time to get back to the Austrian Netherlands. They attacked with an army of 40,000 soldiers on March 18, 1793. In turn, the French could manage only 45,000 soldiers, the majority being raw recruits, under the leadership of General Dumouriez. The result of this battle was a foregone conclusion. The French suffered a shattering defeat, losing around 4,000 soldiers in the bargain. The Austrians lost just half that number. They marched victoriously into Brussels, the capital city of the Austrian Netherlands.

The Siege of Toulon (August 29 – December 19, 1793)

After fleeing from the island, Napoleon's family began to go by the French version of their name—Bonaparte. As ever, Napoleon was full of grand ideas and did not hesitate to make them public. For instance, on July 3, 1793, he suggested a plan for setting up a furnace that could heat cannonballs to such temperatures that they would set enemy vessels aflame within no time. He outlined this plan on paper to France's minister of war. He followed this up with a play, which he wrote in just two nights. The play was in the form of a casual conversation between a royalist and a republican. The dialogues were so clever that the message came through clearly to anyone who cared to understand: it was better to have a Republican government, rather than a Royalist government, for the former was superior to the latter. All the soldiers, workers, ministers and peasants who read the play praised Napoleon.

Napoleon rejoined the French military (the Revolutionary Army) at Nice on June 11, 1793. The revolutionaries executed many Corsicans with glee, since they had rebelled against French leadership earlier, but Napoleon escaped trouble, since he belonged to an obscure province on the island. Therefore, the revolutionary politicians did not feel he represented any danger to them. Similarly, when Napoleon arrived in mainland France, he escaped the guillotine, unlike his unfortunate fellow citizens, thanks to his enthusiastic embrace of the Jacobin faction.

Something else that saved Napoleon's head was his friendship with a powerful fellow Corsican. Saliceti was a deputy to the National Convention, a political advisor and a devotee of the Reign of Terror, wherein numerous executions of all those individuals who supposedly supported the Royals was the order of the day.

When Napoleon rejoined his unit as an artillery captain, he had the task of escorting a special cargo, comprised of gunpowder from Avignon, to a section of the Revolutionary Army stationed in Italy. He had to cross Marseilles, Nice and Toulon along the way. Therefore, Napoleon decided to pay his respects to Saliceti, who was organizing the Siege of Toulon at the time. Toulon, or rather, Toulouse, was important for the French Republic. Located on the south coast of France, it constituted a vital naval base for the country. This place had the advantage of possessing some of the most advanced and heaviest European defenses. The French had to protect it against all costs, for not only were they engaged in wars against other monarchical states in Europe, but also in civil wars amongst themselves. The opposing teams in the civil wars were comprised of revolutionaries and counter-revolutionaries or Royalist forces. The counter-revolutionaries were keen to gain the support of Britain and its allies. They even took the inhabitants of Toulon and Admiral Jean Honore de Trogoff (the Commander of the French Fleet in Toulon) into their confidence. The first to anchor at Toulon's harbor was an Anglo-Spanish fleet commanded by Vice-Admiral Sir Samuel Hood and Admiral Juan de Langara. Soon after, the Sardinian, Spanish and Neapolitan forces arrived, forcing the revolutionaries to launch their siege.

Robespierre, considered by some the intellectual father of the Reign of Terror, was also at the siege when Napoleon arrived. Since the commander in charge of artillery had suffered serious injuries, both the men insisted that Napoleon immediately take over as his replacement. In fact, Saliceti even exclaimed that Napoleon could not have come at a better time. They would go and see General Carteaux, the military general in charge of the siege.

When Saliceti accompanied Napoleon to the battlefield, it became obvious that General Carteaux did not like a young and inexperienced officer stepping in, but had to refrain from commenting in front of two of the most powerful members of the French Revolution. At the same time, it was important to fill gaps in the army. All the nobility, who had served in the French Army earlier, had fled France, for fear of persecution. Therefore, promotions from lower to higher ranks became dependent more upon ability, rather than on birth rank, as the procedure used to be. General Carteaux himself had been a house painter. However, even his staunch patriotism failed to turn him into a good leader for his troops! Regardless, in this particular case, it was clear that mere skill was not solely responsible for Napoleon's promotion. There was also the fact that both he and Saliceti were from the same island. Therefore, desiring to teach the "educated" officer a thing or two, General Carteaux offered to show Napoleon the positions that his army had created for battling the enemy. At the very first battery, he boasted that the English cannons would never reach the French Army. Instead, the French cannons would sink enemy ships, one after another. However, Napoleon, who noticed that the battery was excessively far from Toulon's harbor, requested a demonstration. Even though charged heavily with gunpowder, the cannonball refused to go beyond half the distance. Napoleon was quick to point out the uselessness of setting up such positions. He requested Saliceti give him full control of the artillery.

Napoleon's first act upon taking up command was to carry out a reconnaissance, in order to size up the existing situation and work out a strategy. He realized that the Fort of Equillette was akin to a bottleneck at the mouth of the harbor, since it was located at the extreme end of the French peninsula. It would be a great place for firing cannons from and for preventing anyone from taking up a position in Toulon's harbor. Of course, this angered General Carteaux, who gave Napoleon an earful about his apparent lack of knowledge of geography! Regardless, the enterprising Napoleon went about his work, undeterred. The French Army had no fleet at hand. Therefore, he suggested that it would be good to target the British encampment with French artillery. The encampment was located on a promontory that overlooked Toulouse's harbor. Towards this end, the French would have to recapture Forts Equillette and Balaquier, situated on Cairo Hill. These positions provided a passage between the inner harbor and the outer harbor. If the artillery sufficed to seize control of the harbor, it would force the English fleet to move out to sea. Additionally, the defenders of Toulon would lose their supply line to the sea. This would weaken and confuse the opponents a great deal, thereby helping the French Army to move in and take charge.

General Carteaux fell in with the suggestion, albeit in a half-hearted manner. His attack on September 22, 1793, only alerted the British to the danger. With the help of their allies, they came up with a series of fortifications all around the summit of the promontory. The larger one was Fort Mulgrave, while the remaining smaller ones were Saint Come, Saint Philippe and Saint Charles. The English sailors nicknamed this seemingly unassailable territory "Little Gibraltar." Thus, fate deprived Napoleon of his first victory. Even so, Napoleon's work pleased the politicos and they decided to recommend him for a promotion to the rank of major.

General Carteaux, jealous of "Captain Cannon's" rapid rise to power, decided to thwart all of Napoleon's plans. He refused to grant him infantry support, prompting all the batteries that Napoleon attempted to set up to come to a standstill. As a result, the siege could not progress. A visibly irritated Napoleon spoke with another commissioner of the convention, Barras, insisting that the removal of General Carteaux was the only way to continue the Siege of Toulon. Barras took action and by November 11, 1793, sent in a replacement in the form of General Doppet. This general had been a physician earlier but could not stand the sight of blood! Every time he saw a soldier hit by a cannonball, he would scream at everybody to turn back, because he could not bear to see anymore. Therefore, he left too, although he was honest enough to praise Napoleon to the skies for his active mind and fearlessness. He admired this man, who refused to rest even for a moment, always preferring to stay with his batteries and men. Doppet's replacement was General Jean-Francois Dugommier, an artillery major, an exceptional leader and a trustworthy officer.

Despite his early failures and setbacks, Napoleon, the quick and intelligent thinker, always had backup strategies on hand! His quick response to Little Gibraltar was to position a large battery, nicknamed Convention, right in front of Fort Mulgrave. Then he set up a series of smaller batteries on the surrounding hills, encircling the larger one. He gave these smaller batteries names like Camp of the Republicans, the Men without Fear, the Jacobins, etc. The idea was to motivate the French into giving their best in battle. Amongst all the batteries, the Men without Fear lay in an open and dangerous position. However, gunner after gunner volunteered for the task. This was because Napoleon had the gift of transforming fearful and miserable men into hard, brave soldiers who were proud of their lot. He told them that he wished to create a battery of courageous men who would willingly follow him to enemy positions. Whenever he gave his speeches, his troops, as one man, raised both hands in the air, shouting, "Vive Bonaparte!"

Historians suggest that Napoleon himself stood by the side of this battery, and maybe it is true, if only to prove to the world that all his men were men of courage! The batteries were determined to repel the enemy fleet with the aid of over 300 cannons. Dugommier, who had entered the scene on November 16, 1793, decided that Napoleon was a genius! He exhibited great enthusiasm for executing the proposed strategy. When the Allies became aware of the danger, they came up with a sudden sortie on November 30, striving to capture the artillery. However, the French came up with a counterattack and pushed them back. Napoleon himself engaged in hot pursuit and took the commander-in-chief of the English troops, General O'Hara, prisoner. Despite his capture, O'Hara had nothing but praise for the fearless Napoleon. He admired his courage and intrepidness, suggesting that an army of soldiers such as these would suffice to conquer an entire world.

From December 11 until December 16, 1793, Napoleon and General Dugommier made sure that everything was in place for taking over Forts Equillette and Balaquier. Whenever the artillery attacked, the enemy replied with counterfire. There was an incident to illustrate how gloriously Napoleon inspired his men. During an attack, one of his sergeants, Junot, was noting down a few orders that his leader was dictating to him. At that moment, a cannonball landed just a meter away from him, splattering dirt all over Junot's page. Merely commenting that he would not need sand to dry his ink, the brave Junot continued with his writing! Napoleon smiled at this show of pure and unadulterated courage. Junot would become famous as the Duc d'Abrantes later on.

General Dugommier and Napoleon set the date for the attack on Little Gibraltar as December 16, 1793. At midnight, Napoleon gave the order to begin the assault. The battle continued throughout the night, and by dawn, the French were victorious. In the course of battle, a bayonet wounded Napoleon. Despite his shoe filling with blood, he refused to stop the battle. As soon as Little Gibraltar fell, Lieutenant Marmont, who would become a marshal in the future, battered the enemy forces with their own cannons. Next, Napoleon led the infantry towards the two forts of Equillette and Balaquier.

Even the torrential rain and violent winds could not stop their progress!

Towards the end of the next day, the Allies had lost all their captured forts, including the Fort of Malbosquet. The panic-stricken English raced away to safety, leaving behind their entire set of cannons. The intelligent artillerymen immediately turned these cannons upon the enemy ships resting at Toulon Harbor. The Spanish and English fleets had to burn their arsenal. They retreated, taking along 15,000 inhabitants. As the battle ended, Napoleon threw himself onto the ground, placed a drum under his head as a pillow and fell asleep! His loyal soldiers stayed nearby, ready to prevent anyone from waking him up.

The convention stepped into Toulon on December 18, 1793 and gave it a new name: Port la Montagne. By December 19, 1793, it was all over.

The Siege of Toulon was significant for Napoleon Bonaparte's career. For one thing, though he bravely faced enemy fire during numerous battles, he never received another wound in his life. It was as if fate had decided that he would not be injured or killed until he had fulfilled his destiny. At least, Napoleon believed that. Although a bloody repression followed the Siege of Toulon, Napoleon did not play a part in it. General Dugommier sent in a report about Napoleon's deeds to influential people in the revolutionary government. Therefore, they decided to reward the twenty-four-year-old man with a promotion to brigadier general. He would now be the artillery commander for the Italian Army. Thus, Napoleon Bonaparte had become a celebrity!

While Napoleon was engaged in recapturing Toulon, there was another battle going on elsewhere too. This was in Wattignies, for two days in October. The Allied forces from Britain, Holland and Austria had been busy throughout the summer, capturing various French fortresses. Finally, they decided to take over the garrison of Maubenge. This proved to be a terrible threat to the safety of France, especially to Paris. This garrison not only protected Paris, but also proved to be a wonderful border fortification. Its downfall would have provided the Allies with a large-sized gap for entering France. Noting this, the French mounted a counterattack under the command of General Jean-Baptiste Jourdan. Historians differ on the sizes of the French Army and the Allied forces. Suffice to say that the new recruits of the Revolutionary Army fought with determination and courage, driving the enemy out of France. Even though the casualties were higher on their side, they did not give up and saved the border fortifications from besiegement.

The Events of 1794 and 1795

Napoleon's feats found their way into Augustin Robespierre's written outpourings to his older brother, Maximilien Robespierre. Augustus was very proud of Napoleon. As a result, Napoleon became a commander of artillery in the Army of Italy in February 1794.

While Napoleon engaged in his new duties, the French Republican Army engaged in several battles with the First Coalition forces. It began with the Battle of Tourcoing near Tournai, on May 17 and 18, 1794. Under the command of General Joseph Souham (temporary commander, in place of General Jean-Charles Pichegru), the Armée du Nord attacked the Austrian and British units. The French had the advantage of sheer numbers and were able to force the Austrians, led by Prince Josias von Coburg, and the British, led by the Duke of York, to beat a retreat after two days of hard fighting. The losses were heavier for the Allies, indicating that their plan had failed completely. In fact, the Austrians began to lose all interest in continuing the fight at Western Flanders. As a result, they abandoned the Austrian Netherlands and retreated to an armed camp at Tournai.

The French, emboldened by their recent success and led now by their old commander, Pichegru, decided to carry the battle into the enemy camp. He was confident of victory, since he commanded over 60,000 troops. It was a bloody battle, with the village changing hands at least four times during the day of May 22, 1794. However, the Allied forces were able to hold on to Tournai. Thus, the French were defeated, suffering heavy casualties in the process.

Yet the French Army did not lose heart. The newly constituted Army of the Sambre-et-Meuse, comprised of over 95,000 men and led by Jean-Baptiste Jourdan, decided to capture Charleroi in the Austrian Netherlands. On June 12, the Republican Army placed over 70,000 men in this town. An Austrian-Dutch force with just about 43,000 men attacked on June 16, driving them back over the Sambre River. Undaunted, Jourdan brought his forces back into the fray on June 18. Charleroi finally surrendered to the French on June 26, 1794. Prince Josias von Coburg arrived on the same day, with a large number of Austrian and Dutch soldiers, in order to save the city. However, he was too late. Nonetheless, he decided to attack the French Republican Army.

The Austrian commander divided his forces into five columns for engaging different sections of the opponents' army. However, the French had a trick up their sleeve. With the help of a reconnaissance air balloon controlled by the Aerostatic Corps, they were able to keep track of every movement made by the Austrian Army. At the end of it all, despite a battle lasting well over fifteen hours, and suffering heavy casualties, the French were the victors of the Battle of Fleurus. The Allied forces withdrew from the Austrian Netherlands completely. The French Republican Army reached a decision that day. They would keep up their offensive tactics against the First Coalition as long as it lasted.

The next significant event was the guillotining of the Robespierre brothers on July 27, 1794. The Reign of Terror was at its peak, with Maximilien Robespierre posing as absolute ruler. Discontented voices in the French National Convention turned against him and ordered his arrest. Augustus declared that he was equally guilty of various crimes and would share his brother's fate. Thus, Napoleon's patrons died. The brothers had always shown an inclination to favor Napoleon. Therefore, the convention became suspicious about his loyalty to the Republic of France and ordered his arrest. Napoleon spent a month in prison, starting August 8, 1794. He did fear for his life, but the authorities released him, probably because the reputation he had gained at the Siege of Toulon still endured. After his release from prison, he continued to stay in Paris. However, this was a period of inactivity wherein he received just half his pay. Soon enough, when another royalist uprising seemed in the offing, the convention would enlist his help once again.

Three years had gone by since the formation of the First Coalition. Yet the Allied forces had managed to accomplish little. Over time, the determination and relentlessness of the French Revolutionaries began to wear them down. Sensing this, France initiated certain moves with great diplomatic cunning. It decided to issue separate invitations to the diverse members of the First Coalition for signing peace treaties. The common meeting place would be Basel, a city located on the River Rhine in northwestern Switzerland. It had often served as the best site for peace negotiations, as well as for setting up international meetings. The overseer of all these events would be a French politician and diplomat, Francois-Marie, the Marquess of Barthelemy.

France's first target was Prussia. In actuality, the discussion about a treaty had been in progress since 1794. Without letting the other members know, Prussia had been in acknowledgement of France's ownership over the western bank of the Rhine. Open acknowledgement was possible only when the Imperial Diet (the legislative and deliberative body of the Holy Roman Empire) offered a confirmation. When the First Coalition began working on the impending partition of Poland, Prussia withdrew from it. The country's troops, which had been in place for fighting against Russia and Austria, beat a retreat wherever it seemed appropriate. Therefore, when Karl August Furst von Hardenberg, the Prussian prime minister and statesman, turned up as Prussia's representative, France decided to return all the lands that it had captured on the eastern bank of the Rhine, to Prussia. As a result, the treaty was signed on April 5, 1795.

Surprisingly, both sides never met face to face. Each remained in its own accommodation, passing around the papers to each other via courier. The contract that gave up the left bank of the Rhine arrived in a secret article. Prussia also gave the promise that it would indemnify the right bank of the Rhine, should the left bank ever be covered during a general peace process occurring in France. Peter Ochs, a Swiss politician, behaved as a mediator between both parties, specifically for negotiating the financial aspects. He was also responsible for actually drawing up the treaty. On its part, Prussia honored the Treaty of Basel from May 16, 1795, right up to 1806, after which it linked up with the Fourth Coalition.

France's second target was Spain, whose representative was Domingo d'Yriarte, a Spanish aristocrat (Marques) and diplomat. Once again, Ochs drew up the treaty. According to the agreement, Spain would be able to keep Gipuzkoa if it gave up Hispaniola (the eastern two-thirds of the island) to France. When both parties were in accordance, the treaty was signed on July 22, 1795. By the time of the treaty, the War of the Pyrenees ended. This war had been ongoing between France on one side, and Portugal and Spain on the other, since March 1793.

France's third target was the Landgraviate of Hesse-Kassel. In order to understand this, one has to go back to 1567. At that time, Landgrave Philip the Magnanimous had four sons. He divided the land of Hesse amongst them. Amongst the four Hesse Landgraviates, William IV, the Wise, received the most important, the largest and the most northerly territory. The ruler brought about significant changes in foreign policy matters as well as financial management. The Landgraviate of Hesse-Kassel always supported the members of the First Coalition. Therefore, it was important to get this Landgraviate on France's side. The representative of this Hesse-Kassel, Friedrich Sigismund Waitz von Eschen, came forward on August 28, 1795, to sign the treaty, on the condition that there would be an exchange of captured Austrian soldiers.

Even after the success of the Siege of Toulon, the French Republic had no peace of mind. It was bad enough that the new government battled continual internal power struggles. The sudden uprisings of the royalists at unexpected times did not help matters at all. One such revolt began in October 1795. As the royalist army made its way to Paris, its supporters in other districts joined in along the way. They even managed to take over a particular area of the city, Le Peletier. Comprehending the danger, the governing body of France summoned the National Guard and an improvised army of patriotic revolutionaries. However, their attempts to quell this uprising failed. The government wondered what would happen if the revolt succeeded due to an increase in numbers. They were terrified! Just then, Brigadier General Napoleon Bonaparte arrived at the convention. He had come to offer his assistance in controlling the rioters. However, he had a condition. No one should interfere with his actions. The National Convention agreed. Napoleon prepared himself to face the royalists on October 5, 1795.

At 1:00 a.m., Napoleon refused to follow the ineffective orders of the men in charge of the National Convention's forces. Instead, he ordered a cavalry unit to fetch forty cannons from a specific place in Paris. When they arrived, he assembled the cannons on the route that the royalists would take during their advancement. The group arrived at this location at 10:00 a.m. Its numbers were huge, while the Republican Army was small. In fact, the ratio was around 6:1. However, Napoleon had positioned his guns very carefully. He was using canisters of grapeshot as weapons. The cannons did the job wonderfully well, since Napoleon had positioned them at close range to the attackers. Within two hours of vigorous fighting, he had defeated the Royalist Army. Hundreds lay dead on the streets, while the remaining fled. Napoleon's horse died too, shot from underneath him. However, he survived, unscathed! Murat, the cavalry major, retrieved whatever was left of the artillery. With this whiff of grapeshot, Napoleon began his subtle fight to overthrow the French Republic and become the future emperor of France!

Napoleon Acquires a Wife (March 8, 1796)

His intelligent handling of the royalists' revolt against the Directory (a five-member ruling committee of France at that time), impressed everyone. Paul Barras, one of the Directory's members, invited Napoleon to a party. He wanted to use Napoleon's military skills for both his personal and political benefits. Towards this end, he decided to palm off his current mistress (Marie-Josephe-Rose de Beauharnais) onto Napoleon. After all, Napoleon needed a wife. In actuality, Barras was tired of Rose and was keen to acquire her best friend as a new mistress. He could not afford to keep both of them. Therefore, without revealing his plans to Rose, he requested she attend his party and entertain the brigadier general as best as she could. She was to express a deep interest in him and enthusiastically praise his talents.

Rose followed Barras' instructions beautifully. Napoleon was highly impressed that such a beautiful and wealthy member of the old aristocracy was so interested in him. When Barras urged him to request her hand in marriage, Napoleon acquiesced. Barras assured the young brigadier general that Rose was a great catch, with all her wealth. She would definitely make a perfect wife for Napoleon.

Although Rose was much older than Napoleon, he was so infatuated with her that he paid no attention to the age difference. He did tell her, though, that he hated her name and would henceforth call her Josephine. When Barras advised her to give in, Josephine refused. Barras informed her that he had a new mistress and could not afford to look after Josephine too. If she refused to marry Napoleon, he would no longer provide for her. As a result, she would be put out on the streets along with her children, Hortense and Eugene. A disturbed Josephine then agreed to marry Napoleon. She would not be able to give him any children, since she had been barren for some time. However, she did not let Napoleon know this fact. Soon enough, the couple wed. When Napoleon took over as the commander-in-chief of the French Army in Italy, on

March 11, 1796, just two days after his wedding, he had no choice but to depart for Italy.

In actuality, the National Convention did not have its eye on Italy. Instead, it was aiming to target Germany. However, the group wanted Napoleon out of the way, for fear of him causing some kind of trouble in the future.

When twenty-six-year-old Napoleon reached Nice on March 27, 1796, he found a large group of disgruntled soldiers, intent on mutiny. They were short of funds, shoes, equipment, rations and supplies. Then again, all the men were not new recruits. There were quite a few experienced individuals who were just waiting for an inspiring leader to guide them. Regardless, new or old, no one was ready to listen to Napoleon. They felt that he had risen in the ranks not through the exhibition of any kind of heroism, but through mere favoritism. All that he had done was fire his cannons at a mob in Paris and marry the discarded mistress of one of the most influential members of the Directory. Quite a few felt that he did not look like a general at all and expressed amusement at his eagerness to show off the portrait of his newly acquired wife. However, when Napoleon put on his general's hat and began to ask all kinds of questions about positions, strategies, etc., everyone's opinion underwent a quicksilver change!

In fact, Napoleon proved to be exactly the tonic that the dispirited Army of Italy needed. He managed to win their hearts via his oratory. Napoleon declared that he understood what they were going through, especially as the French government owed them much, but could give nothing. These soldiers had revealed plenty of patience and courage in different battles on harsh terrain. Yet they remained devoid of glory and riches. Now that he had arrived as their leader, he would lead them towards riches, glory and honor via the capturing and raiding of rich provinces and opulent towns. However, he needed assurance from them that they were neither lacking in endurance nor bravery. After all, they were a mere 37,000-40,000 men in the face of combined enemy forces of more than 50,000 men.

He was also well aware that, apart from the immediate problems that they were facing, the French Army had to battle all manner of environmental conditions too. For instance, there was the area lying between two big mountain ranges which became the theater of operations for the army in Italy. As the River Po flowed from the mountains to the plains, it tended to gather more water along the way. Therefore, by the time it reached the Adriatic Sea, the river appeared quite swollen. The flow of this river was parallel to the general line of Napoleon's operations. Since the French Army possessed no pontoon trains or boats, and there were hardly any bridges in place, it found it difficult to tackle watery obstacles at times.

As for the roads, they were definitely not too trustworthy either! The only road for communication was the one traversing Genoa to Nice along the coastline. It was quite rugged and narrow at some places. Then again, its positioning was such that the ships, which had command of the sea, could find targets to fire at quite easily. The enemies of the French Army were lucky since they had access to good roads on the rich plains. As for the towns and cities, there were quite a few of them. Although their politicians either favored or disfavored the French, the common citizens tended to remain neutral. They changed their sympathies in alignment with the changing fortunes of war. However, many of these citizens derived some kind of inspiration from the novel ideas resulting from the French Revolution.

After his speech, Napoleon set about ordering fresh supplies to Italy. He also wielded a firm arm against deserters. Overall, he managed to impress upon the men that he was determined in both speech and action. Thus, throughout the entire campaign, Napoleon demonstrated that by offering motivated leadership, taking care of the needs of an entire army of men and practicing solid strategies and tactics, it was possible to turn an entire group into an excellent offensive machine. It was something that no other French commander had been able to achieve before.

Now, what was Napoleon's Italian Army like?

For one thing, the stronger demi-brigades of battle was comprised of 3,000 men, while the lighter ones were comprised of anywhere between 1,000 and 1,500 men. When four demi-brigades came together, they comprised a division of the infantry. The infantry carried flint guns, which happened to be extremely effective at 180 yards. These guns could target opponents at 500 yards with ease. The men could fire two rounds within a minute. Every soldier had fifty rounds with him. The artillery wagons that followed the infantry carried more weaponry with them. With regard to the reserve divisions, they comprised around 3,000 to 4,000 men. Each division of the cavalry was comprised of five regiments. Twelve-pound guns, each with a range of around 1,500 yards, accompanied the battalions. The range was reduced to 500 yards if case shot came into play. For every 1,000 men, there were three to four guns. While two went along with the battalion, a couple remained in reserve. However, during Napoleon's campaign in Italy, he had the guns separated from the battalions and linked with batteries, instead.

Until Napoleon came along, the French cavalry appeared inferior to that of Austria. However, he took charge and changed everything. Nonetheless, what made the French Army so different from the armies of other nations? To begin with, these soldiers preferred to travel light, taking whatever they could from the land around them. Therefore, lengthy trains carrying supplies or magazines did not follow them around, hampering their progress. Every man carried whatever he could, to last at least three or four days. Just a few wagons came behind the marching soldiers, filled with medical supplies, packets of biscuits and ammunition.

Despite all the hardships, the French possessed amazing powers of endurance! They refused to let fatigue stand in the way of motivation. Instead, they remained enterprising, active and supremely intelligent. It helped that they were eager for glory, thanks to Napoleon's constant and timely appeals. Then again, thanks to their experiences during the peak of the Revolution, these men knew how to be flexible in their fighting formations. As a result, they always managed to catch their opponents by surprise! In fact, the army's sharpshooters did not have to confront any kind of competition during this campaign at all, for the opponents found it difficult to be as agile and mobile as the French were! Napoleon went out of his way to bring about healthy cooperation between the French inventory and

French artillery. Above all, regardless of rank, many young and enthusiastic men had become officers. These unexpected elevations only served to fuel their eagerness to show off!

The leaders, who were there to help Napoleon Bonaparte, were heroes in their own right. For instance, there were three experienced divisional commanders. The oldest was 53-year-old SZrurier, who had had earlier served the Royal Army for 34 years. He tended to be on the gloomy side! Augereau was only 38 years old, but an extremely accomplished swordsman. MassZna, highly popular with the men, was a very capable tactician, renowned for his victory in the Battle of Loano. He had already seen Napoleon in action at Toulon, when battling alongside the brigadier general. Apart from the trio, there was Louis-Alexandre Berthier, chief of staff. Flamboyant Joachim Murat was the cavalry colonel, while August Frederic Louis Viesse Marmont would take over as artillery expert. Geroud Christophe Michel Duroc, A. E. F. de La Harpe, Jean Andoche Junot, Claude Victor-Perrin Victor, Jean-Baptiste Cervoni, Jean Lannes, Francois Macquart, Louis Gabriel Suchet, Pierre Dominique Garnier, Antoine Guillaume Rampon, Jean-Baptiste Bzssi res and Bartholemy-Catherine Joubert were other noteworthy members of the French Army.

The aim of the French Republic was to separate Sardinia-Piedmont from the First Coalition. However, this could be possible only if Napoleon's army defeated the Sardinian and Austrian armies. Additionally, Napoleon could not afford to keep every single man by his side to be part of his field force. He had to leave a sufficient number in charge of guarding the vulnerable supply lines that stretched along the Italian Riviera and the French Riviera. The battleground included mountain passes, river valleys, towns and connecting roads.

It was to Napoleon's advantage that the armies from Austria and Piedmont hated each other! If these armies had united, they would have outnumbered the French Army greatly, and even defeated the heroes in rags! General Jean Pierre Beaulieu was still the active commander-in-chief of the Austrian forces, despite being 72 years old. He had 19,500 soldiers under his command, positioned at Alessandria in the north. There were another 11,500 Austrian soldiers under the care of General Eugen Graf von Argenteau, stationed at Acqui, as well as occupying the outposts stretching from Carcare to Genoa. As if these troops were not enough, 20,000 Piedmontese soldiers, under the command of General Michelangelo Alessandro Colli, were waiting to tackle the French, all the way from Ceva to Cosseria. It helped that General Johann Provera of Austria was nearby, along with his troops, to come to their aid, albeit only if necessary. In general, the Austria and Piedmont troops preferred to remain hostile to one another, thereby permitting the French to instigate one against the other and emerging as the winner every time!

Napoleon's first targets were General Colli and his troops. He wished to drive them out of the way. After studying the maps carefully, along with Berthier, he realized that the town of Carcare was the central link between the Austrians and the Piedmontese. If he hit the place successfully, his army would attain numerical superiority over each adversary. Towards this end, he made his plans carefully, intending to put them into action on April 15, 1796. Several troops would move in different directions, thereby confusing the enemy forces and forcing them to tackle the French at diverse places. For instance, Augereau and MassZna would take their men to Carcare. SZrurier would proceed to Ormea and engage the Piedmontese. A group under the command of Garnier and Macquart would offer a demonstration before Cuneo. While Harpe and his men moved towards Sasello, Cervoni's men would travel to Voltri.

However, Napoleon took some precautions too. He decided that, unlike the others, Cervoni and his group would reach Voltri long before, as an advance guard. At the same time, Napoleon requested that neutral Genoa's senate grant the French Army permission to pass through its terrain. When news of Napoleon's actions reached General Beaulieu, he decided to launch a surprise attack on the enemy at Voltri on April 10, 1796. At the same time, he sent another group of soldiers, under the command of General Argenteau, to Savona through the Bormida Valley and Carcare. He wanted to trap the soldiers beating a retreat from Voltri.

He was not to know that this was exactly what Napoleon wanted! The brigadier general had no worries about Cervoni and his men. Even if caught by surprise, Cervoni would manage to beat a masterful retreat from Voltri, which he did! At the same time, Napoleon was well aware that the Austrians had built a number of fortifications on the mountains, just northwest of Savona. They would not allow General Argenteau and his men enough time to get there and trap Cervoni's retreating men. In fact, Argenteau showed up at Montenotte in Savona on April 11. By that time, Napoleon's forces were in place.

On April 12, the French hit the Austrian forces from the front and the flanks. Suffice to say that the Austrians found themselves on the run. They had to retreat towards the north of the mountains, towards Dego, losing a large number of soldiers. Even the Piedmontese Army was unable to advance and had to remain static. This was Napoleon's first victory, causing him to believe that he was destined to achieve greatness. In turn, the French soldiers discovered that their morale had received a superb boost.

On learning that the French had vacated Voltri and General Argenteau had been defeated at Montenotte, General Beaulieu decided that he would move to Dego. There, his troops would join Argenteau's group, and befriend the Piedmontese Army. However, it would take him some time to reach the place. Napoleon knew this by studying the maps and decided to use the time to focus on the Piedmontese Army. He gathered over 25,000 soldiers by bringing together the entire divisions belonging to Augereau and SZrurier, and part of the division under the command of MassZna. They would attack from both the left and the right. At the same time, a group (with MassZna in charge) would march across the hills to Dego, where they would not allow Argenteau to regroup his soldiers and interfere with the French thrust against the Piedmontese Army.

Nonetheless, things went a little awry on April 13. As had been decided earlier, Augereau successfully attacked the left flank of the Piedmontese army at Millesimo that morning. In fact, he was able to push it towards Montezemolo and advanced towards the ruins of Cosseria Castle. However, it was here that disaster struck. General Provera was waiting with his small group of Austrian soldiers (around 900 of them) at the castle. They engaged in a lively battle, thereby preventing MassZna and his soldiers from launching their attack on Dego. Napoleon had been very clear that MassZna would not make his move until Cosseria Castle had fallen. Thus, a precious day was lost. Regardless, when noon of April 14 approached, MassZna refused to wait any longer and attacked the Austrians at Dego. He received dramatic and heroic help from the dragoons under Murat's command! As a result, the French were able to take the majority of the 5,000 Austrians prisoner and captured nineteen guns.

As for Cosseria Castle, it finally fell, clearing the way for the French to attack Colli's troops openly. They made their way to Ceva, believing that they had won the battle at Dego. Unfortunately for MassZna and his men, who had remained at Dego, they had not reckoned with the cunning of the Austrians. While the French engaged in plunder and foraging for food, leaving their positions unprotected, five Austrian battalions under the leadership of General Philipp Vukassoviac, arrived on April 15. They completely routed the enemy, even taking all their guns. MassZna himself barely escaped in his nightshirt!

Napoleon could do nothing but cancel his plans for Ceva. He returned to Dego with a reserve force. Finally, after 1,000 casualties on the French side, Napoleon recaptured Dego. At the same time, Augereau and SZrurier hounded Colli's troops until they had no choice but to settle down in Ceva. From here, the Piedmontese troops were able to repulse a premature attack by Augereau on April 16. In fact, the French suffered heavy losses. Therefore, Napoleon decided to leave La Harpe's men in charge of Dego, while SZrurier and MassZna joined Augereau, along with their troops. Now, Colli's army was under threat from all sides! He beat a hasty retreat to Mondovi.

The French troops followed the Piedmontese Army, ensuring that they had no way of communicating with their Austrian allies. In retaliation, Colli had his men destroy all the bridges and set up stone fieldworks. Nonetheless, his actions did not deter Napoleon. He urged his infantry and soldiers to attack the Piedmontese Army from all sides on April 20. The Piedmontese troops fled to the plains of northern Italy, pursued by the French. Thus, the French took Mondovi.

This latest victory became the turning point of Napoleon's campaign that he had initiated just ten days ago. His next halt was Cherasco, where he would come into direct confrontation with King

Victor Amadeus II of Piedmont. However, on April 23, the monarch requested peace terms. This resulted in the Armistice of Cherasco on April 28, 1796. According to this diplomatic move, the monarch could keep his throne, as well as his independence, provided he handed over the fortresses of Alessandria, Tortoni and Cuneo to the French. The first two fortresses would allow the French to conduct operations against Austria's large army in northern Italy with ease. Cuneo would keep his lines of communication open with his base in the south of France. Napoleon also wanted Piedmont to grant unrestricted right of way to French messengers, who had to keep transferring messages between France and Italy all the time. His third condition was that the captured lands in Nice and Savoy should remain in the possession of the French.

Back home, the French Directory felt that the armistice was too lenient in its terms. However, Napoleon was keener to make his campaign against Austria a success. He needed the help of King Victor Amadeus II for keeping the rear of the French Army safe. It was enough that Piedmont left the First Coalition. Thus, Napoleon had found a way to keep track of every enemy movement in order to fulfill all the promises he had made to his army on March 27, 1796.

Numerous Battles with Austrians

Soon after signing the Armistice of Cherasco, Napoleon took time to reorganize his troops. Austrian General Beaulieu took the opportunity to evacuate Alessandria and crossed the River Po. Napoleon's Army now numbered 36,000, as Generals Garnier and Macquart had joined him, along with their respective troops. The French wished to cross the River Po too, but they could not do so with an alert Beaulieu on the other side. Therefore, instructing SZrurier and MassZna to engage in diversionary tactics at Valenza, where the Austrians had crossed the river, Napoleon decided to move to a place fifty miles away. The French would cross the River Po at Piacenza. A group of select grenadiers, the Corps d'Elite, under the leadership of General Claude d'Allemagne, would rush ahead and set up a bridgehead there.

As had been predetermined, an advance guard of four battalions moved to the northern bank of the river on May 7, 1796. Beaulieu, however, received news of the crossing and hastily sent across two generals to attack. In the violent conflict that occurred the next day, General La Harpe lost his life. Therefore, the chief of staff, Berthier, took over the command of the French Army. Beaulieu decided to cross the River Adda at Lodi. Napoleon followed him. When the French arrived there on May 10, they discovered that the Austrians were safely across the river. Additionally, around 10,000 men and a dozen cannons awaited the arrival of the French on the bridge. The first charge at Lodi, undertaken by Napoleon and his grenadiers, failed. However, the second one was successful.

Napoleon hoped that the French Directory would appreciate his efforts. He also hoped to show them what he was truly capable of, during future battles. Unfortunately, for him, the Directory was terribly jealous of the brigadier general's successes and decided to split the command of the French Army between Napoleon and General Francois ftienne Christophe Kellerman. They sent a dispatch on May 10, to which Napoleon replied that it was better to have one bad commander in place, rather than two good ones. He sent along a large convoy of plunder too! Naturally, the Directory backed down.

Kellerman forwarded 10,000 reinforcements, one being his own son. A month later, Napoleon entered Milan in triumph. He received a hero's welcome, but his popularity waned as both the French government and the French Army engaged in plunder of supplies, cash and art treasures. Napoleon left Milan on May 22 in order to pursue Beaulieu. However, he had to return after two days, in order to put down local revolts in both Pavia and Milan. On May 30, the French Army attacked

Borghetto, thereby scattering the Austrian forces. This success inspired Augereau, SZrurier and MassZna to continue the pursuit, while capturing various cities/towns along the way. Beaulieu and around 4,500 of his men had no option but to enter the imposing fortress of Mantua. The fortress boasted a garrison of 12,000 men and 316 guns.

The French were unable to overcome Mantua on May 31. However, Napoleon himself came under a sudden attack on June 1, at the village of Valeggio. He barely managed to evade his enemies by vaulting over a few garden walls! Nonetheless, his brave commanders managed to station their cavalry in Mantua by June 3. Napoleon spent the next few weeks collecting large cannons, as well as art treasures from diverse places, prior to planning for a siege of Mantua.

The First Battle of Altenkirchen took place on June 4. General Jourdan and General Kleber, with 22,000 men, engaged with Austrian Prince Wurttemburg's army of 24,000 men. Despite having less men, the French Army divided itself into three groups for maneuvering the Austrians out of position. The Austrians fought hard but could not defeat the determined French. They had to retreat, yielding vital supplies and magazines to the enemy.

Thereafter, on June 19, the French engaged with 13,000 men under the command of Austrian

General Kray, at Ukerath. In actuality, the French Army of the Sambre and Muese, under the command of General Jourdan, was retreating from the line of the Lahn River as the Austrians gave chase. At that moment, General Kleber, who was in charge of the rearguard, decided to teach the Austrians a lesson. Unfortunately, he received a lesson that day! The Austrians were superior in cavalry and could fight very hard when pressed! While 1,500 French soldiers died or received wounds, 700 became captives of the Austrians.

The next battle was at Kinzig (Rechen) on June 28. The French Army, comprised of 34,000 soldiers, tangled with 17,000 Austrian soldiers under the leadership of General Sztarry. The daring French had managed to take a bridgehead across the River Rhine via stealth. This was opposite Strasbourg at Kehl. They battled the Austrians, who were holding onto their strong position along the Kinzig River. However, the Austrians could not hold out for long, as reinforcements did not arrive.

An Austrian field marshal, Graf von Wyrmser, who replaced Beaulieu, arrived on June 29 with 50,000 soldiers to take over Mantua. Dividing his forces into three groups, Wyrmser marched ahead. The central forces dislodged MassZna from Verona. The western forces battled with Augereau on the shores of Lake Garda. An extremely concerned Napoleon ordered every available soldier to the northern front. Regardless, he had to abandon the siege of Mantua, leaving behind the guns that his Army had captured earlier at Tuscany. The French rear was exposed, and Napoleon felt that defeat was certain.

While Napoleon was engaged in his own battle, General Moreau and his group of 34,000 soldiers pursued the Austrian forces that had retreated from the River Kinzig to the River Murg, at Rastatt. Once again, the Austrians could not stand up to a determined French Army, especially one under the command of Moreau!

The Battle of Ettlingen (Malsch) took place on July 9. Moreau's 65,000 men outnumbered the 40,000-strong Austrian Army, commanded by Archduke Charles. It was a bloody fight, with neither side giving in. Since both sides lost an equal number of men, the battle was tactically a draw. However, the Austrian Army could not hand a decisive defeat to the French Army. Therefore, viewed strategically, the Austrians were on the losing end.

Another battle took place on July 14, the Battle of Haslach. This time around, General Frolich, of the German Allied force, brought along 15,000 men skilled in cavalry to fight 20,000 French soldiers under the leadership of General Ferino. The Allied forces sought to keep the French out of the Black Forest. The French pushed in the Allied center around Haslach, thereby forcing the flanking forces to retreat. This defeat affected the Austrian lines of communication, making the Austrians feel that it would be better to fall back on the Danube, rather than on the Rhine.

Coming back to the Siege on Mantua, Napoleon concluded that, given enough time, it would be easier to engage with every wing of the Austrian Army separately, thereby preventing them from regrouping. For instance, Wyrmser enforced a delay at Valeggio, which lasted three days. This helped Napoleon place Augereau in position on August 3, such that he engaged fellow generals Wyrsmer and Lipthay in battle. This way, they could not go to the aid of a third general, Quasdanovitch, whose troops were fighting a losing battle with MassZna's men. On August 5, the Battle of Castiglione commenced. Napoleon created three divisions from 30,000 men and commanded them to attack Wyrmser's 24,000 men at Castiglione from all sides. Around 2,000 Austrians were wounded or died, while 1,000 became prisoners. The Austrians also lost 120 caissons and twenty cannons. The survivors survived only because three days of continuous fighting had left the French Army completely exhausted!

On August 7, the 46,000-strong French Army of the Sambre and Meuse, under the command of General

Kleber, attacked a 40,000-strong Austrian Army under the leadership of General Wartensleben. This time, the target was the Fort of Forcheim. The defeated Austrians could only move southwards and eastwards.

August 11 was the Battle of Neresheim. Once again, it was Moreau in command of 50,000 men. The Austrian Army, under the leadership of Archduke Charles, was in a stronger position. He had 55,000 men at his command. The archduke decided to create multiple converging columns in order to engage the French Army scattered along the upper and middle Rhine. The idea was good, but the actions were poorly coordinated. Additionally, it was raining and the roads were muddy. While the French Army on the left gave way, the men on the right and in the center held on energetically. Thus, it was a no win-no lose situation!

The Battle of Friedberg, along the length of the Lech River, took place on August 24, once again with Moreau in command of 53,000 soldiers. General Latour had 34,000 Austrians under his command. The river had swollen due to the recent rains. The Austrians were in a strong position, yet the French Army had initiative and courage. Both sufficed to bring the Austrians to their knees and forced them to move towards Isar and Munich. However, this was a strategic mistake on Moreau's part. His men were going deeper into Bavaria, as the archduke was defeating General Jourdan in the north. To illustrate, General Jourdan and the French Army of the Sambre and Meuse, comprising 45,000 men, had a face-off with a 63,000-strong Austrian Army led by Archduke Charles, on August 24, at Amberg. The French experienced attacks from the front, flanks and rear. They had to retreat north and west, thanks to the poor condition of the roads.

True, the French Army suffered defeat. Yet it saved itself from being trapped or disintegrating. This defeat boosted the morale of the Germans. As if this defeat was not enough, General Jourdan's men suffered another beating at the hands of Archduke Charles' Austrian Army on September 3, at Wurzberg. Apart from the Austrians possessing excellent cavalry skills and light troops, they had the support of the local populations too. The people were becoming very angry at the frequent French depredations. Jourdan's army took up a position on the heights of the right bank of the Main River separating Wurzberg and Schweinfurt. The French Army's losses were heavy—2,000 men and seven guns. Thus, the French Army of the Sambre and Meuse experienced a complete rout and destruction.

Leaving his leaders to take care of other things, Napoleon continued his Siege of Mantua. While 10,000 soldiers handled the siege, another 3,000 guarded Verona. The main army, comprised of 33,000 men, continued to pursue Wyrmser. His army thought of making an entry into Tyrol, which Austrian troops were defending, on September 4. However, when Napoleon learned that Wyrmser was returning to Mantua, he gave up that plan and continued his pursuit. The Battle of Bassano began on September 8, when Colonel Lannes' soldiers dove through the Austrian lines and stormed into town. Pursuing the fleeing Austrians, Murat's cavalry seized two pontoon trains, thirty-five guns and five colors. The French took 4,000 Austrians as prisoners.

While many of the survivors fled to Frious, Wyrmser returned to Mantua on September 12. He brought reinforcements with him. However, the city garrison found it difficult to feed 23,000 men, since food supplies were dwindling. The French Army did not find itself in a happy situation either. France was slow to send reinforcements. Additionally, around 14,000 men among the 41,000-strong army fell sick. Even SZrurier fell sick. Therefore, Napoleon appointed various groups to guard entry points towards Lake Garda, Verona and Bassano. For his part, he took up administrative matters. For instance, he decided to unify Italy via the formation of three republics. One would be Cisalpine, with Milan as the focal point. The second would be Cispadene, with Reggio and Modena as important centers. The third would be Transpadene, combining Ferrara and Bologna. Over time, he would bring all the three states under one unified North Italian Republic. However, the well-connected, the church and the nobility were not willing to fall in with his ideas.

While Napoleon engaged himself in this manner, the French Army of the Rhine and Moselle, under General Moreau's leadership, engaged in three battles with the Austrians. The Battle at Bilberach, on the banks of the River Riss, on October 2, was comprised of a tussle between the French Army and 23,000 Austrians under the command of General Latour. Although forced to retreat in the initial stages, Moreau's men set up a fierce counterattack and escaped a pursuit by Latour. The next meeting took place at Emmendlingen on October 19. This time around, the person in charge, Archduke Charles, managed to push the French Army out of all but a tiny slice of Germany, Schliengen.

The French Army lacked numbers when the Battle of Schliengen began on October 23. Moreau had to withdraw across the Rhine at night, since the Austrian troops pushed the French Army out of Germany. Although a clear winner on the surface of it all, Archduke Charles lost the strategic war. He could not recapture the bridgeheads at Kehl and Huningen or destroy the French Army.

After noticing the minor and major skirmishes resulting in minor or major victories, Napoleon received a terrible shock when he encountered a clear defeat for the first time during his campaign in Italy. The Austrian Army returned with reinforcements in November, along with more experienced leaders. They attacked the French Army at two places simultaneously—Bassano and Trent. However hard the French soldiers fought, it was of no use. The Austrians emerged the clear victors by November 4, as they captured Trent, Rovereto, Bassano, Vicenza and Fontanove. A shocked Napoleon decided that some "talking to" was in order. He visited Rivoli, where the shaken troops and their leader, Vaubois, were gathered. Rebuking them for not exhibiting constancy, courage or discipline, Napoleon suggested that they had allowed themselves to fall prey to cowardice. He declared that they were neither French soldiers, nor men belonging to the army of Italy. This was enough to make every soldier vow to conquer or die!

Over the next few days, there were several bitter conflicts. On November 12, the French Army captured two villages. However, the Austrians managed to recapture them once again, along with 750 prisoners and two cannons. The French Army lost 2,000 soldiers. A chastened Napoleon retreated to Verona, wondering how he would overcome this defeat.

He informed the Directoire in France of their predicament, suggesting that he and his brave leaders were probably fated to die. Though the French Army felt abandoned in Italy, Napoleon never stopped encouraging the troops as much as he could. He declared that even if the enemy troops were more in number, the French Army could gain everything by making just one determined effort. To show that he meant what he said, Napoleon decided to attack the enemy's rear, similar to what he had done at Lodi and Bassano. He decided that Vaubois and 3,000 men would suffice for guarding Verona. The rest would have to join him.

On the night of November 14, Napoleon and 18,000 soldiers moved towards Ronco, in order to take a pontoon bridge spanning the Adige River. Chief Engineer Antoine-Francois Comte AndrZossey had it ready by November 15. Augereau crossed first, to make his way to Arcola, while MassZna crossed the river next and moved to Porcile. MassZna was able to defeat Provera's advance guard and take Procile. However, when Augereau was crossing, he encountered two battalions of the Croatian Infantry with their guns sweeping the roadway. A desperate Napoleon, realizing that they would not be able to catch the Austrians by surprise if they kept losing time like this, grabbed hold of the colors. He held the flying banner high as he boldly led Augereau's troops forward. Obviously, it led to a whole lot of firing and confusion, wherein the general even fell into a canal. However, his aides-de-camp saved him from the bayonets of the Austrian counterattack. The French captured Arcola at seven in the evening, but it was too late to capture Austrian General Alvintzy. He had escaped. At the same time, Napoleon received news of the French Army losing Verona. Thus, he had to give up Arcola for the moment.

The next day, Napoleon attacked Arcola once again. It was in Austrian hands, along with the recaptured Porcile. The determined French Army got Porcile into its hands for the second time. On November 17, the French fought viciously, forcing both Austrian generals Alvintzy and Davidovitch to retreat, one after the other. By November 21, the French had gained 1,500 prisoners, two bridging trains and nine cannons. Thus, the third counteroffensive by the Austrians, failed. Upon getting this news, the French Directoire initiated negotiations with the Austrian monarch. When suggestions about sending provisions to Mantua entered the discussion, the negotiations stopped. Therefore, the Directoire sent reinforcements for continuing the Siege of Mantua.

While all this was going on, Alvintzy had ordered reinforcements too, similar to Napoleon. He remained at Bassano, along with 45,000 soldiers. He decided to divert the brigadier general's attention by launching attacks on Augereau and MassZna, on January 8. He did not touch the Lake Garda sector at all, which made Napoleon suspicious. Then he received the news that Alvintzy was moving towards Adige Valley with 28,000 men. The idea was to deliver Napoleon a crushing defeat. Napoleon left 3,000 men to guard Verona. The rest of the French Army accompanied him to Rivoli. His army was lucky, for the roads going north were in good condition. The Austrians were not so lucky, since just a couple of roads were ideal for moving artillery and men. Thus, they found maneuvering highly difficult.

At the first sign of daylight on January 14, the parties launched the Battle of Rivoli. The Austrians planned to surround Napoleon on all sides. However, the French Army was prepared this time. Not only did the troops drive the enemy away from Rivoli but they also managed to hold on to the southern sector. While the Austrian Army was still reeling from these attacks, Napoleon's entire army moved in the northern direction and separated the Austrian forces into two divisions. With the arrival of reinforcements, the French were even able to take 3,000 prisoners. When the battle was almost at an end, Napoleon requested Joubert take over. Accompanied by MassZna, he moved south, in order to prevent Provera's large army from reaching Mantua. With Szrurier also joining in, Provera had no option but to give in. Only 16,000 of the original 30,000 men remained. They surrendered to the French Army.

Finally, the French Army gained Mantua on February 2, 1797. Within a span of five days, Napoleon had reduced the Austrian forces to 13,000 fugitives. There had been 48,000 fierce fighters earlier! An angry Archduke Charles set about assembling at least 50,000 men in two regions— Tyrol and Frioul. Napoleon did not bother to wait for reinforcements. Instead, he worked out a strategy for enforcing a two-pronged preemptive advance on Vienna. From March 1 until April 6, the French Army, under the command of diverse leaders, hounded the Austrians, until one town/city after another fell into its hands.

General Hoche had taken over the French Army of the Sambre and Meuse. After crossing the regions of Dusseldorf and Neuwied, he surprised the Austrian commander, General Werneck, and his army of 40,000, when they were still in the process of working out a strategy! The French chased the Austrians all the way to the gates of Frankfurt, until information about peace negotiations filtered through to all of them.

This time, General Moreau was in charge of 60,000 men belonging to the French Army of the Rhine and Moselle. This army was about to confront 17,000

Austrians under the leadership of General Sztarray. The advance groups in Moreau's army crossed the River Rhine in boats. Other soldiers waited on a pontoon bridge, in order to deal with the Austrians and their counterattacks. This battle was successful, for the French took possession of the bridgehead at Kehl once more. Hostilities ceased because peace talks were underway.

The peace negotiations between France and Austria got underway on April 18. This was the opening of the Preliminaries of Leoben. After several months of talks, France and Austria affixed their signatures to the Peace of Campo Formio on October 17, 1797. According to the conditions outlined in the treaty, the majority of French conquests received maximum importance. For instance, France created the Ligurian and Cisalpine Republics in northern Italy. Furthermore, Venice's Ionian Islands in the Adriatic Sea belonged to France now. Austria received Venetian territory that lay to the east of the Adige River. It also received the city of Venice, Dalmatia and Istria. This was in compensation for what Austria had lost in Lombardy. As a result, 1,100 years of Venetian independence ended. Austria handed over its Belgian provinces to France.

Pending ratification at a congress of the estates of the empire, Austria agreed to permit France to annex territories that lay on the left bank of River

Rhine, stretching from Basel to Andernach. Mainz appeared in the picture too. France promised Austria that it would use all of its power to ensure that both Salzburg and a part of Bavaria reached Austrian hands. Both parties agreed that Prussia would receive no territorial compensation. The agreement remained a secret between France and Austria. Thus, apart from Britain, which continued to remain hostile towards France, the rest of the members of the First Coalition preferred to have peaceful relationships with Napoleon Bonaparte's country.

When the French Directoire began to suspect that it was becoming unpopular in France, it sent for Napoleon. The members told him to instruct some troops, under the command of a general, to protect the legislature at Tuileries. On September 4, 1797, General Pierre-Francois-Charles Augereau separated over 130 counter-revolutionaries and royalists from the Corps Legislatif. He also ensured that several nonjuring priests, deputies, journalists and even the director (Marquis de Barthelemy) were deported to Guyana, South America. Although the royalists lost once again, the Republican Constitution did not have its earlier strength either. Furthermore, the French Army had become the new power of the nation. This was sufficient to pave the way for the entry of Napoleon's military despotism, in the near future.

The First Coalition comprised some of the most powerful nations in Europe at that time. In contrast, the new French Republic was a hotbed of internal strife and controversies. Furthermore, it was near bankruptcy. Yet this nation had succeeded in defeating the members of the coalition in an intelligent manner. This became possible because the members of the coalition failed to function harmoniously as one. Despite being part of a group, each country wanted to work independently of the others.

Even the objectives of the various members of the First Coalition did not appear to be similar to one another. For instance, Britain wanted to expel the French Republic from The Netherlands. This way, it would be able to make that province secure for Austria. However, Austria wanted to recover The Netherlands, prior to exchanging it with Bavaria. These kinds of thoughts did not find favor with the British government. As for Prussia and Russia, they were keen to see Poland partitioned. They were not interested in helping Austria win over France. The British were only interested in obtaining Dunkirk for themselves. Therefore, they besieged it. Similarly, the Prussians had their eyes on Poland, prompting them to remain on the Rhine for a long time. The Austrians wanted a hold over Lorraine and Alsace.

Since each nation was only focused on its selfish aims, the Allied forces could not function as one or even comprehend the danger presented by France. Thus, there was no unity of purpose at all. Ultimately, this proved fatal. For example, it would have helped if all the members of the First Coalition had come together to advance upon Paris as a single team. Instead, each Allied power was only keen to establish its control over all the frontier fortresses of France.

According to the Allied mindset, France was struggling with a revolution. Therefore, it would be wonderfully easy to defeat it. However, everyone failed to realize that no one was keen to fight with the Bourbon monarchy. Instead, they were up against a nation striving to live up to the ideals of equality, liberty and fraternity. Since not a single nation could rise above its petty jealousies and selfishness, it failed to defeat France. Paradoxically, the very cruelties witnessed during the French Revolution had also served to keep the people united against them.

The Allied powers of the First Coalition were not interested only in France. They were keen to begin a revolution in Poland. In fact, Russia and Prussia could not wait to see the country partitioned and grab their shares from the bits and pieces! Poland did undergo partitioning in 1793, and both the nations were overjoyed at receiving their portions from Poland. After 1793, Poland underwent another division in 1795, losing its status as a separate state. Many patriotic Poles fled the country. They came together in Italy to form the Polish Legion. The leader of this legion was General Jan Dabrowski. This legion linked up with Napoleon's army in France's fight against the Austrians. The legion even came up with a special song, which would become liberated Poland's national anthem later on. Currently, however, the legion's efforts to liberate its homeland went in vain

Austria, Russia and Prussia shared the rest of Poland. Even during the sharing process, the members of the First Coalition strove to gain a greater share than the others did. This kind of mindset could only paralyze and defeat, instead of uniting. The French Army sensed this, especially with Napoleon at the forefront. Therefore, it was able to plan, strategize and act with wisdom, patience and courage.

Napoleon and his Italian Campaign

Napoleon's heroics during the lengthy campaign of Italy, and the determined fighting abilities of his intelligent assistants, such as Augereau, Murat, MassZna, Szrurier, Joubart, etc., did not go unnoticed. The officials at the top recognized that Napoleon had three outstanding qualities, which had repeatedly helped to turn sure defeat into victory. One such quality was his mastery over initiating tactical offensives. He had the ability to think on his feet, coming up with brilliant strategies every time a crisis occurred. In fact, he believed in being on the offensive, rather than being on the defensive, the majority of the time. Secondly, Napoleon utilized the central position brilliantly, in order to force an enemy to retreat. Finally, he knew how to concentrate all the forces at the right place and at the right time. This was what had prevented the Austrians from wresting Mantua from the French, not just once, but four times! As a result, the chief of the Topographical Bureau (Ministry of War), General Henri Jacques Guillaume Clarke, found it necessary to discuss Napoleon at length in the report that he forwarded to the French Directoire. According to the general, people loved, respected and feared Napoleon, all at once. All agreed that he was a military genius. The general praised Napoleon for his enlightened ideas, perceptive judgments and well-calculated methods of execution. Obviously, this was a man with superior talents, and future generations would continue to gain inspiration from him.

Yes, the French Directoire did acknowledge Napoleon's greatness. After all, he had done the impossible, bringing the various members of the First Coalition to their knees and ensuring that France won many battles. Regardless, Napoleon would not let anyone forget any of his good deeds! He had a huge ego. He commissioned two newspapers to write about his successful exploits at home as well as abroad. As long as he was outside Paris, he continued to send updates about whatever was happening. Therefore, the whole of France was obliged to know and recognize him! At the same time, he commissioned a few artists to celebrate his achievements. His rising popularity made the members of the National Convention slightly uneasy. They feared that he might become too popular for comfort, specifically as 1798 promised to be a quiet year! The members of the First Coalition, barring Great Britain, had made their peace with France. Nonetheless, they had no reason to worry. If anyone thought that Napoleon Bonaparte would settle down to a life of peace and comfort after his campaign in Italy, he/she was sadly mistaken! Despite being short in stature, Napoleon had tall ambitions! He decided that he had to tackle the African side of the world now. He was in Toulon at that time, and the target was Egypt.

Originally, Egypt had been under the rule of a dynasty of slave warriors, the Mamluks. In fact, the Mamluks had taken control of the kingdom from its earlier rulers, only in 1250. When the Turks, belonging to the Ottoman Empire, arrived in Egypt in 1517, they were not able to destroy the Mamluks. Despite being in the Ottoman system, the slave dynasty managed to remain in control of large areas of Egypt. Over time, by the beginning of the 18th century, the Mamluks had almost returned to power in the country. However, their lack of unity proved to be an obstacle for garnering strong centralized rule in Egypt. There was severe infighting amongst the Mamluk households. Finally, the Qazdagli faction proved to be the winner in 1765. Even then, the conflicts continued. In 1775, the winner of a terribly violent conflict died. As a result, the whole kingdom descended into chaos. The followers of both factions again divided themselves into two main factions. Each faction had two leaders in charge. In 1778, the faction under the control of Ibrahim Bey and Murad Bey proved victorious. However, it was as if fighting and quarrelling was in the blood of these slave warriors. They would pretend to reach a consensus on peace agreements, and soon after, break their promises!

Although the fighters reached a more permanent understanding amongst themselves by 1785, it was too late. Murad Bey had often threatened foreign merchants who brought foreign revenue (taxes) into Egypt. This time around, in 1786, he attacked the merchants of Alexandria. The angry merchants then approached the government of Istanbul. The government welcomed this move, for it was keen on launching an expedition that would help it get back control of Egypt. The expedition reached Egypt in July 1786 but merely succeeded in driving Ibrahim Bey and Murad Bey out of Cairo. The refugees found a haven in Upper Egypt and the Ottoman commander took over Cairo. His government recalled him in 1787.

Over the next four years, Ibrahim Bey and Murad Bey controlled the southern part of Egypt, while Ismail Bey retained control of Cairo. Unfortunately, for them, a plague hit Cairo in 1791. Ismail Bey and the majority of his supporters died, leaving the way clear for Ibrahim and Murad to return to the capital city in August 1791. Even the Ottoman sultan decided to pardon them. Nonetheless, these men could never give up their habits of bickering all the time or charging outrageous taxes from all those who wished to trade with Egypt. As a result, Egypt lost almost all its business well-wishers, including the French. Nonetheless, Ibrahim and Murad found it highly difficult to contain their greed, even going so far as to inflict it on an entire populace. Rosetta and Damietta had been prosperous once. However, they lost over half their population over time. Even Cairo's population shrank by 40,000 people. As for Alexandria, it was almost in ruins. But it did not matter. Ibrahim Bey and Murad Bey only wanted to increase their personal fortunes.

France's Original Intentions and Plans

Since Egypt's rulers had affected their trade, the French were angry with them. Therefore, they decided to seize the entire colony of Egypt. They were confident of their success, believing that the populace would feel grateful to them as their liberators from the wicked Mamluks. Even the Ottomans would not mind tolerating the French presence in their domain, if it meant getting rid of their subjects, who were misusing their independence. This revolution would be akin to the one that the French citizens had initiated. There would be modernization and development in Egypt, with the creation of novel institutions after discarding the old. Of course, all this would depend upon the Ottomans remaining neutral. The French hoped that the Ottoman Empire's anger at the behavior of the Mamluk rulers would overweigh its anger at an ally's invasion of what was officially its province.

In reality, the ambitious French would not be content to stop at Egypt. They hoped to challenge their eternal enemy, the British Empire, not at its home base, but in faraway India. In fact, the French were still furious with the nations involved in the Seven Years War, which had successfully destroyed France's influence in India. While all this was music to Napoleon's ears, his personal ambitions stretched far beyond what the French government had envisioned. For one thing, he wanted to make Malta his own. Under the control of the Knights of St. John, Malta would prove appropriate for a French naval base. As for moving to India, Napoleon wanted to dig a canal through the Suez, wherein French fleets would find it easy to enter the Red Sea. As for Egypt itself, predominantly Islamic in culture, Napoleon hoped to gain the country's favor by proclaiming that the French believed in God much more than the Mamluks did. Furthermore, he would also declare that the French were true Muslims. However, this would come into play only if religion became a major issue during his conquest of Egypt.

Obviously, despite his youth, Napoleon had a conviction that he could conquer the world. According to him, Europe was too small. Ultimate greatness lay in conquering the East. After wresting Egypt from the Ottomans, he would proceed to India and expel the British from there. Then, he would attack the Greeks, destroy the Ottoman Empire, raise a storm against Constantinople and finally, finish Europe via rear attacks. Oh, Napoleon could work out grand plans indeed!

The French maintained strict secrecy as far as the mounting of an expedition to Egypt was concerned. The preparations, however, proceeded at tremendous speed! By April 12, everyone of importance had approved it. The preparations took ten weeks. Napoleon set sail for Egypt on May 19 or 20 1798 (there's historical confusion about the exact day). He ensured that they halted at ports, such as Genoa, Marseilles, Corsica, Civitavecchia, etc. along the way, thereby increasing the level of secrecy even more. Even the men on board did not know about their actual destinations until they were well out to sea. Thanks to Napoleon's cunning, by the time the news of France's new target reached Great Britain via French newspapers, it was July 12. Vice-Admiral Nelson of the British military was in the Mediterranean region at that time. However, even he could not catch up with the speedy French fleet as quickly as he would have liked to!

Napoleon raised a huge army for the expedition. It had scientists and cultural experts too, along with the ablest of Napoleon's generals (Murat, Marmont, Junot, etc.). Even Alexandre Dumas, the famous French novelist, joined the expedition. Apart from all the above, there were 167 savants. These savants would prove to be the nucleus for the formation of a novel Academy Egypt. The diligent academicians did amazing research and came up with amazing discoveries! For instance, they found the Rosetta Stone, which, in turn, led to the deciphering of Ancient Egyptian hieroglyphics. This would let the world know more about Ancient Egyptian history.

At the same time, it was doubtful if the army was large enough to tackle the entire Ottoman Empire and bring Egypt permanently into France's possession. In any case, France would be free to move around in the Mediterranean region and reinforcements would arrive. Getting back to the original size of the French Army, it included 2,800 cavalry, 30,000 infantry, two companies of miners and sappers, sixth field guns and forty siege guns. France decided that this would do for the initial conquest, even if the army had to stretch its equipment and capabilities somewhat. Then again, realizing that transporting everything to the specified destination would not be easy, the French government supplied thirteen ships, seven frigates and almost 300 transport ships.

One may wonder why Napoleon was so keen on taking the Island of Malta, since Egypt was more of a priority at that time. Was Napoleon becoming addicted to seizing power wherever he could, just because it was there for the taking? In actuality, there was a valid reason for his desire to annex Malta to France. The process had been set in motion several years earlier but was about to bear fruit under Napoleon's command.

Going back in history, the Knights of St. John had been without a permanent home since 1522, ever since the powerful members of the Ottoman Empire had driven them out of Rhodes. When Charles V was in power in Spain in 1530, he feared that the Ottomans would attack Rome. Therefore, he requested the Knights protect him, in exchange for living on Malta. Thus, the Knights had been able to make Malta their permanent home from 1530 onwards. As soon as they took up residence, they set about fortifying their new domain, as well as making Italian the official language on the island. These were the years of the Crusades, and therefore, the Knights deemed it their duty to provide medical assistance to everyone. Towards that end, they had numerous hospitals constructed, all displaying the eight-pointed cross. However, were their enemies, the Turks, belonging to the Ottoman Empire, going to stay quiet for long? They followed the Knights and laid siege to the island, beginning May 18, 1565. The battle was terribly violent and bloody. However, the Knights, along with the people of Malta and 8,000 Sicilian soldiers, fought long and hard. Ultimately, they emerged winners.

The head of the Knights at that time, Grandmaster de la Vallette, gave orders for a new and strong city to rise on Malta. The walls would be high, similar to those in a fort, and all manner of protective strategies were initiated, in order to avoid another siege. Unfortunately, the grandmaster did not live long enough to see his dream city reach completion. Over the years, other grandmasters took over. They had other cities built and put in place new fortifications. They looked after the sick and continued to construct medical schools and hospitals using funds obtained from France, where they had administrative districts belonging to their order. Thus, the Knights of St. John were exceedingly wealthy. By the time 1789 came around, around two-thirds of this order was comprised of people belonging to the French nationality.

Everything was going well until the French Revolution began and France severed its trade links with the Knights. By August 1789, the new French Republic abolished all titles. Everybody was just a citizen. On July 30, 1791, the revolutionaries, who were in power, passed a new order. The order declared that every French citizen affiliated to any kind of chivalric order that had its origin beyond the boundaries of France would be denationalized. In other words, France would no longer view these members as French citizens. On September 19, 1792, the legislative body in France took away all the

Commanderies, deciding that they would prove useful to the nation. As a result, the Knights of Malta lost half their revenue. The government sold off the confiscated property. France's expansion of its rule over North Italy and other places across the globe resulted in the order losing still more land. They tried to make up for it via the creation of a new langue, but it did not work. Then, they tried to enhance their revenues from other parts of Europe, and even on Malta itself, but nothing worked. They could not even go back to the original source of revenue, which they had practiced in earlier days—piracy.

The Knights had no more problems with the Ottoman Empire, though, for a peace accord had come into existence in 1796. Napoleon approached the French Directoire on May 26, 1797 and suggested a conquest of Malta. He felt that the island would prove to be an important pawn in the Mediterranean region strategy, where the final target was the destruction of the British Empire in India. Apart from serving as an important point for France's naval base, Malta would also prove useful for securing the supply lines during his campaign for Egypt.

The French Army, comprising 50,000 men, reached Malta on June 9, 1798. The men were under the command of Admiral Brueys at that time. It was the tradition in those days to permit only two ships from a belligerent fleet to enter the harbor of a neutral state at any given time. However, Napoleon did not place a request. Instead, he demanded that Baron de Hompesch, the order's grandmaster at that time, allow the entire French fleet to enter Malta's Grand Harbor simultaneously to load fresh water supplies. However, the grandmaster was suspicious of Napoleon's true intentions. He declared that he would allow only two to four vessels to enter the harbor at a time. The French commander decided to utilize this rejection as the perfect excuse to initiate hostilities. He was well aware that the grandmaster lacked resolve and the capacity to make quick decisions. In fact, the grandmaster simply retired to his palace, lacking the backbone to confront the aggressive Napoleon! Furthermore, the inhabitants of Malta tended to be rather passive by nature. Even the Maltese forces were small, comprising just 332 Knights, 13,000 militia and 3,600 men in the harbor. When the French Army initiated action at four diverse areas on June 10, 1798, the grandmaster and his men could offer little in the way of resistance.

The main aim of the French forces was to isolate the city of Valetta, a fort that acquired its name from past Grandmaster de La Valetta. Towards this end, one group under the command of Desaix decided to take over Marsaxlokk Bay first, prior to crossing the

Cottonera lines and then attacking the main gates of the fortress. Another group, commanded by Vaubois, decided to land on the coastline stretching from Sliema to Qawra Point, enabling it to take over Medina and all its surrounding villages. D'Hilliers and his group would go for St. Paul's and Mellieha Bays. From there, they would assist Vaubois in taking over Medina, as well as Madliena Heights. The fourth group, under the leadership of Reynier, would take over the Island of Gozo.

The four attacks that the French initiated that morning lasted only until the afternoon. The French captured the entire Island of Malta, barring the Marsamxett and Grand Harbors, as well as Fort St. Lucian. The Knights could not do anything much, since they were fighting amongst themselves. Some Knights, who were of French origin, declared that they would not fight people from their own native country. The native Maltese then chose to initiate a revolt. Since the grandmaster and his Knights could not tackle both war from outside and war from the inside, they capitulated on June 12, 1798.

As was his usual wont, Napoleon grabbed all the treasures he could from Maltese churches and the Knights' libraries. He had them stored on his ships. On the positive side, he initiated a series of reforms, despite being on Malta only for six or seven days. To begin with, he ensured the abolition of all religious orders, including the Knights of St. John. He abolished their privileges, feudal rights and the right to encourage slavery on the island. All Turkish slaves became free to lead their own lives. Napoleon also initiated a civil code, reformed the tax system and gave orders for the modernization of the hospitals and university. While all this was fine, there had to be someone in charge to make sure that implementation took place in an appropriate manner. Towards this end, Napoleon set up a government commission and divided the Island of Malta into twelve municipalities. Every municipality would have its own judge. The administration would take care of public finances too.

However, his best reforms pertained to the field of education. Laying down the principles himself, the commander of the French forces suggested that fifteen primary schools be created. With regard to secondary education, an école centrale took the place of the University. Eight chairs, with an extremely scientific outlook, would take care of education in the arenas of algebra, arithmetic, geometry, physics, mechanics, chemistry, navigation, astronomy, stereotomy (science and art of giving particular shapes to three-dimensional solids) and stereometry (measurements of the volumes of diverse three-dimensional, solid figures). Above all, he selected sixty children, aged between nine and fourteen, belonging to Malta's wealthiest families for receiving a good education from colleges in Paris and other places in France. Prior to leaving, he left 4,000 soldiers in charge of guarding this new acquisition. Thus, Napoleon engaged in a mixture of plunder, reform and military rule, whenever and wherever France emerged as a winner.

The Battles

As mentioned earlier, Nelson's fleet was in the same region at that time. However, he was having a run of bad luck. It began with his flagship, the HMS *Vanguard*, losing its masts in a severe storm, on May 20. In fact, the ship almost ran aground. However, Nelson's determined tactics managed to keep the ship safe. Regardless, the captains of his various frigates felt that it would be necessary to move to Gibraltar for major repairs. As a result, they returned themselves, leaving Nelson stranded without frigates. Any fleet, without frigates, tended to be weak. Behaving as the eyes of the fleet, these frigates were capable of enhancing the region of visibility or doubling the area of visibility on the open seas. Towards this end, they could out-sail the main ships or sail at the limits of visibility from the main ships. In their absence, Nelson could see the sea, as far as the highest mast on his ship would allow. Regardless, he was hoping to sight French ships sometime or the other. He was not to know it then, but his fleet would come quite close to Napoleon's fleet on the night of June 22-23. In fact, Nelson's fleet was faster and overtook the slower French transport ships, without even being aware of it. As a result, the French did hear signal guns from the British ships passing by.

Nonetheless, Napoleon did not believe that any British fleet of significance could be around and refused to call an alarm. After passing Napoleon's fleet, Nelson's ships touched Alexandria on June 29. There was no news of the French. Therefore, he began to wonder if the French Army had actually been heading towards the west, wherein they would be able to put their plans into action without English interference. The frustrated Nelson decided to sail towards the north, thereby missing Napoleon by a couple of days.

Napoleon had learned that Nelson was in the Mediterranean region. Then again, he was well aware that the Nile would flood in August. Therefore, he was also fighting against time and had to get things done as quickly as possible. His fleet landed on the Egyptian coast on July 1. The leaders in his group suggested that they continue their journey until they reached the Rosetta mouth of the Nile River. However, Napoleon decided that it would be wiser to capture the Port of Alexandria first. After all, this place had a small garrison and was not capable of handling the French Army. Thus, with the help of 5,000 men who landed close to Alexandria, Napoleon captured the port city on July 2, 1798. Once Alexandria was in his hands, Napoleon asked the rest of his force to land on the shores of Egypt too.

Surprisingly, the arrival of the French did not rattle the confidence of the Mamluks at all! They did not really know the potential of Napoleon's French Army and felt confident that they could tackle this foreign invasion quite easily. They had confidence in their military abilities, as evinced by Murad Bey's decision to gather together 6,000 of his best cavalry and counterattack the invaders. In addition, there was an Egyptian force on standby, comprising 24,000 men and 30 guns. A Mamluk commander was in charge of this rather poor-grade infantry. In contrast, the French Army of the Orient numbered around 28,000, with Brigadier General Napoleon in command. Although the march to Cairo had not been easy, with Egypt undergoing an extremely dry season, prior to the flooding of the Nile, the French survived. They had not given in to the heat. Additionally, they had confronted several Bedouin raids along the way quite successfully.

The French Army was inferior as far as its cavalry was concerned. Therefore, Napoleon divided his forces into five large squares. He named these divisions Desaix, Bon, Dugua, Vial and Reynier. They stretched from the left to the right, from near the Nile River to the desert flank. The squares integrated every bit of the artillery within them. They also were sufficient to protect any rear elements that appeared vulnerable, by keeping them within their boundaries. The battle began on the banks of the Nile, which was opposite to Cairo and within sight of the pyramids, on July 21, 1798. The Mamluk cavalry initiated it, midafternoon. Although the Mamluk cavalry did its best, it could not hold its own against the superior French inventory squares of Desaix and Reynier. The French had much better discipline and firepower than the Egyptians did. They did not engage in wild dashes like the Mamluk cavalry.

The defeat took place at Shubrakhit. Similarly, squares Vial and Bon attacked the village of Emabeh, where the Mamluks had left the majority of their inventory and guns. It was a foregone conclusion that the troops would face slaughter at French hands. While the French lost about 300 men, or a little more, the Egyptians lost around 5,000 men. The majority of the defeated troops included a majority of Mamluks. The French were ecstatic, for they could engage in rich looting. Napoleon was happy to gain command of Cairo and the majority of Lower Egypt.

Napoleon did not know that Vice-Admiral Nelson was hunting for him. The admiral had been mortified to discover that he had missed the French Fleet earlier and had permitted it to land on Egyptian shores! His fleet roamed the seas from the southern coastline of Crete to Syracuse in the eastern Mediterranean region. When the British ships had touched Syracuse on July 19, Napoleon had been very near Cairo. Regardless, Nelson concluded that the French fleet was definitely somewhere in the eastern region only. Therefore, he began to head towards Greece. During the journey, on July 29, he received the news that he had been waiting for, for such a long time. He urged his fleet to head towards Alexandria for the second time in three months. When his ships reached Alexandria on August 1, 1798, they found the French transports anchored at Abu Qir Bay. Admiral Brueys was in charge of thirteen ships and four frigates. The British also received news about the French warships when the masthead of one of Nelson's warships managed to spot the former's sails. The private ships moored at Alexandria managed to confirm the numbers and locations of these warships.

Nelson had come fully prepared to tackle the huge French fleet. While his fleet had been looking for signs of the French fleet, he had engaged in discussions with his captains about methods to deal with the French. He was well aware that their army had the skills to deploy itself in diverse ways. Nelson wanted his teams to be prepared to deal with every kind of French deployment. He made it explicitly clear that he would go for a direct attack on the French Army, regardless of wherever he found it. In case he had no choice but to fight at night, he would do so, using prearranged signals and means of identification. In case he found the French fleet at anchor, he would strive to force his leading ships to move between the Egyptian shores and the French ships. Keeping all these thoughts in mind, as soon as Nelson spotted the moored French ships at Abu Qir Point, at around 4:00 p.m., he knew what he had to do. His fleet would forget about the French rear and instead attack the center, as well as the French van. True, it would be night within almost three hours. Yet the British fleet, comprised of fourteen ships and seven frigates, launched its attack immediately.

Captain Foley, who was in charge of the HMS *Goliath*, realized that there was a gap between the Alexandrian coastline and the French ships. At least, part of the British fleet could sail into this gap. As a result, the French ships, in the front and center, found themselves sandwiched between two lines of British ships. One line lay on the shore side, while the other lay on the seaside. The French rear did not even enter the picture! The Battle of the Nile cost the French 1,700 men, eleven ships and two frigates. Additionally, around 1,500 men received injuries. In contrast, the British lost just 218 men. Around 678 required medical help. They did not lose even a single ship. However, there were slight mishaps. For instance, one English ship ran aground. A French flagship exploded in a spectacular manner.

Nelson's men ensured that prisoners captured by the French received their freedom. Napoleon received the news about his fleet's annihilation even while he was preparing to enjoy the fruits of his conquests. His Army of the Orient felt completely cut off, since the Mediterranean had become a British lake. France could send no reinforcements, thereby depriving Napoleon of both men and supplies. In the absence of these reinforcements, he would not be able to put his plan for the East into action. Napoleon strove to move his heavy siege guns by sea to Syria. However, the British captured those guns and turned them against the French themselves. Nelson also made sure to send a vital message to India. He wanted the British in India to know that they need not fear the French anymore. The British had delivered one of the most crushing naval victories of all time to the French!

The Mamluks might have been defeated in the Battle of the Pyramids, and the majority of their forces might have been on the run, but their determination to retake what was theirs still existed. Ibrahim Bey had run away to Palestine. Murad Bey had taken the remnants of his force and retreated towards Upper Egypt. Over the next ten months, General Desaix and his French forces prevented the Mamluk army from threatening the French occupation of Lower Egypt. In fact, the Mamluks allowed the French to sense their presence, but managed to evade capture at their hands at the same time. As a result, the French Army had no choice but to split forces, in order to tackle Murad Bey and his men. Therefore, Upper Egypt continued to remain under the control of Murad Bey, disrupting the supply of grain to Lower Egypt. The French had to acknowledge this fact in later years.

Similarly, the local people were not about to accept a French presence in Cairo so easily. Even the Ottoman Empire was not keen to have the French occupying their soil. Furthermore, the destruction of the French fleet on August 1, by Nelson's Fleet, emboldened the locals. They began to show evidence of this by fortifying the strong points in and around Cairo, specifically the Great Mosque. They also began distributing weapons across the streets. The French resorted to brutal and swift methods to put down these October revolts, even if it meant taking to street fighting. In just two days, 3,000 Egyptians lost their lives, while the French lost around 300. The dead included General Dupuy, the French commander, and Joseph Sulkowski, Napoleon's aide-de-camp. This was because the sheikhs and imams urged them to be merciless with the invaders, whether they encountered them at home or on the streets, all the while citing this as the will of the Prophet. They even circulated a manifesto throughout Egypt, suggesting that the French were stubborn infidels who looked upon the Old Testament, the New Testament and the Koran as fables. Soon, their numerous forces would arrive by land and sea, in order to overcome Egypt. Therefore, it was necessary for the people to remove every single vestige of this foreign presence, in order to please God or the Lord of the Worlds.

Even Napoleon found it difficult to enter the city via its gates, for the crowd repelled him. Therefore, he took a detour and entered via the Boulaq Gate. Obviously, conquering and holding on to Egypt was not as easy as Napoleon had thought it would be! It was a critical time for the French. They could not even ask for reinforcements, since Nelson had destroyed their entire fleet. If that wasn't enough, the British were engaged in menacing the coastal towns. Murad Bey was roaming free in Upper Egypt. As for Lower Egypt, Generals Dugua and Menou could barely hold onto it. The British, Murad Bey, the Egyptian peasants and the Arabs were fighting for a common cause, which was driving the French invaders back to where they had come from.

Deciding that enough was enough, Napoleon instructed that cannons be set up in the citadel in Cairo. The cannons fired at Azhar, as well as the areas around it. The forces would enter these areas at night and destroy the barricades. Soon, the French cavalry was able to make its way into Azhar and killed many people. The French Army then forced the Arabs to retreat to the desert and turned its artillery onto the rebel city of Cairo. Napoleon went on a personal tour of the streets, prompting the rebels to hide in the Great Mosque. Declaring that their god was too late, and he would finish what they had begun, he ordered his army to storm into the building. Breaking down the gates, the French stormed inside and initiated a massacre. Over 5,000 rebels lay dead or wounded at the end of it all.

Once through, Napoleon took over as absolute ruler of Cairo. He sought out the instigators of the revolts. As soon as he was convinced of the participation of an Egyptian, Turk or a Sheikh, he had the individual executed. Not yet satisfied, he decided to initiate a high tax as punishment too. The divan had to give up his position to a military commission. Finally, Napoleon sent his men around the cities of Egypt to post a proclamation. The words on the proclamation suggested that the people stop placing their hopes and faith in Ibrahim and Murad. Instead, they should place their trust in a person who engaged in creating men and empires.

Formation of Second Coalition (December 29, 1798)

Napoleon's bold moves had been causing anxiety to several European monarchs all this time because the French ambitions to bring diverse parts of the world under their control threatened to destroy vital commercial links. However, the defeat of the French forces at the hands of the British offered a ray of hope. As a result, several nations came together to initiate the Second Coalition in December 1798. This coalition would last until 1801, comprising the Vatican, England, Portugal, Russia, Turkey, Naples and Austria. It decided to launch a three-pronged attack against the French. While Britain attacked them through Holland, Austria would confront them through Italy. Russia would attack them through Switzerland/Helvetian Republic. The Second Coalition wanted to bring France to its knees, since not only Napoleon, but also the French Directoire, were doing their best to stir up war throughout Europe. For example, France had ensured that it deported the pope to its shores, while it set up the Roman Republic. Then again, the Directoire had converted Switzerland to the Helvetian Republic in alignment with the French model and had placed some troops there to protect it. This was not all. The French Army had even attacked the Kingdom of Naples, in order to create the Parthenopean Republic. Finally, the French had exiled the king of Piedmont-Sardinia, in order to annex both parts of the kingdom to France.

Now Napoleon's eyes were on Syria. Buoyed by their navy's victory over France's troops, British diplomats at Istanbul took immediate action! They urged the Ottoman Empire to fully oppose the French. Therefore, the empire declared war against France on September 9, 1798. It decided to attack by both sea and land, thereby pushing Napoleon's troops into confronting two separate Ottoman armies. The first was the Army of Damascus, which would move through Palestine and Syria (modern Israel) in order to launch an attack on Egypt across the Sinai Desert. The other one, the Army of Rhodes, with the help of the friendly British Royal Navy, would make a landing near the River Nile. Naturally, the French would find themselves surrounded, as well as outnumbered.

However, they had underestimated Napoleon's intelligence. He had been expecting a Turkish attack on Egypt. Therefore, he decided on a preemptive attack upon both Syria and Palestine. Towards this end, he gathered a field army of 13,000 men and initiated a march eastward on February 6, 1799. Moving towards Syria, the French Army took over the coastal towns of Al Arish, Gaza, Jaffa and Haifa, defeating the Mamluks, Arabs and Turkish groups along the way. Of course, the French troops did meet with stiff resistance, but ultimately emerged winners through sheer persistence. For instance, the Al 'Arish garrison refused to give in for eleven days. Jaffa (now Tel-Aviv) was a different matter altogether. There were 3,000 men in the garrison who managed to hang on from March 3 until March 7. What followed the surrender was probably one of the most shameful incidents witnessed in the Napoleonic Wars.

The aggression of the French soldiers reached a terrible high during the assault of Jaffa. Around 2,000 Turkish soldiers came forward to give up but the French soldiers used their bayonets freely upon them. Then they turned their ferocity upon the inhabitants of the town. They did not spare even the women and children. Instead, they went around town, robbing and murdering whomever they met. This insanity continued for three days until Napoleon put an end to it via a repulsive act of his own. He decided that the 3,000 men in the garrison would prove to be a burden on the French Army. He could not spare men to look after these prisoners of war, nor could he afford to feed them either. Therefore, he decided it would be best to execute all of them, which he did, without any remorse. The atrocities of the French Army only served to make other Ottoman garrisons decide to resist the enemy as long as possible.

While the French were crowing over their victories, it was as if a divine hand decided to punish Napoleon's soldiers. Hundreds of them became afflicted with the bubonic plague. They complained of sudden rises in body temperature, headaches, delirium and swollen lymph nodes under their arms (buboes). The disease attacked the lungs, liver, spleen and lymphatic system, killing the patient within 24 hours. French doctors took action as soon as they realized they were dealing with a dangerous plague. Even if they refused to tell the soldiers the truth, the men themselves knew what was happening to them. Only Napoleon was calm, believing that moral courage was the need of the hour. He believed that fear of the disease caused it to spread even more rapidly than usual. Therefore, he made a personal visit to the hospital, in order to talk to his soldiers. He stayed there for almost two hours, talking with every soldier who was conscious and could hear him. He even took note of all the administrative details, helping wherever he could. His talk had the desired effect, for his troops felt less fear and experienced a boost in their flagging morale.

Three days later, Napoleon gathered the rest of the army and marched towards Haifa, and later, Acre. He left 150 soldiers, with a general in charge, to look after 300 soldiers afflicted with the plague. Unfortunately, the plague followed the French Army wherever it went, even across the desert sands of Egypt. Terribly worried about the survival of his army, Napoleon ordered that the remaining patients be poisoned. When the doctor refused to give the requisite doses of laudanum, the pharmacist took over. Around fifty or so patients died. Historians suggest that by the time Napoleon sailed for Europe on August 24, 1799, over 2,000 soldiers had died due to the bubonic plague.

Siege of Acre (March 17 – May 20, 1799)

Napoleon wanted to take over Israel/Syria and annex it to the permanent colony which he had set up in Egypt. He also wanted to weaken the Turkish land forces within the next two months. After that, he would have to rush to Alexandria to prevent the Turkish Navy from landing on its shores. With these plans in mind, he took along 13,000 men and began a march around the eastern edge of the Mediterranean Sea. The French Army arrived at Haifa on March 17, 1799. From this area, it was possible, via a telescope, to spot the Citadel of Acre, which had been the victim of several wars during the Crusades. However, when he looked through his telescope, Napoleon received a shock! There were Turkish gunboats and British battleships resting in the harbor. They seemed to have control over all the sea-lanes in that area. This meant that they had seized his transport ships bearing all the heavy siege guns.

The British had been thrilled to discover that Napoleon had sent his siege train by sea and had promptly captured the entire artillery! This also meant that Napoleon would not be able to receive any news from his base camp in Egypt or from France. However, the new Alexander the Great, as he believed himself to be, pressed on. On March 18, his army found itself positioned in front of the walls of Acre. The citadel, which lay on a promontory, was surrounded on all sides except one, which faced land. Additionally, a neat harbor nestled alongside the citadel. The French initiated their Siege of Acre upon the former capital of Israel/Syria on March 19, 1799.

Pasha-el-Djezzar had been the governor of Acre for over 25 years. He had earned the sobriquet of Djezzar (butcher/cutter) due to his savagery with people he considered his enemies and talked quite a bit about treating the French with the same kind of savagery if they dared to set foot on his land. However, when they did arrive at the Citadel of Acre, he felt that he had no choice but to abandon his post and the citadel. He would have abandoned his people if Captain Sir William Sidney Smith of the British Navy had not been there at that moment. Smith talked the governor out of leaving his post.

Instead, he urged Djezzar to confront Napoleon Bonaparte. One could understand the governor's fears. When Daher el-Omar, the original ruler of Acre, had erected some fortifications, he had ensured that they could confront every kind of enemy force. However, the people of Acre had neglected to fortify Acre's defenses for many years. Therefore, the citadel would not be able to withstand a violent siege.

After asking a team to conduct a thorough inspection of Acre, Captain Smith decided to add his own small naval squadron to the bulk of the Ottoman garrison in that area, in order to tackle Napoleon's forces. He had to do something about the defenses of the citadel too, for the team's report suggested that it was almost impossible to defend Acre by land; this could only be accomplished by sea. Therefore, soon after he arrived in Acre on March 15, 1799, he asked Louis-Edmond Phelippeaux-Smith, a French engineer, to reconstruct the wall.

Those who knew Naval Officer Smith, a rival of Vice-Admiral Nelson, tended to view him as courageous, intelligent and flamboyant. In 1798, the French had captured him and placed him in the high-security Temple Prison of Paris. This was around the time that Napoleon was requesting permission from the Directoire for his expedition to

Egypt. Despite his incarceration, Smith operated an efficient spy ring from his prison cell. He even inscribed a personal message for Napoleon on the walls of his cell. He congratulated Napoleon for being at a high level in his career, while Smith himself remained at the lowest level in the same. However, he was confident that the wheel of fortune would soon turn, wherein he and Napoleon would exchange places. He even taunted the brigadier general about having to occupy the same prison cell one day, long after Smith had left it.

With the help of some French royalists, the naval officer made a daring escape from prison on April 24, 1798. Soon after his return to Great Britain, he took up command of Tigre, an eighty-gun battleship. The British dispatched him to Constantinople (Turkey) in October 1798. He was to ensure that Sultan Selim of Levant (East Mediterranean region) received sufficient protection against Napoleon's French Army. In fact, the sultan had declared war on France and wanted Smith to take charge of the forces at sea. The sultan himself would take control of his land forces. Thus, Smith was around when Napoleon's army entered Acre. He understood Napoleon's mindset well and, when Captain Smith sought his assistance, ordered the digging of counter tunnels all along the northeastern tower. These tunnels would aid in demolishing the tunnels dug by the French soldiers and would help prevent a conquest.

Captain Smith had another advantage. As mentioned earlier, his men had taken over the siege artillery from France's captured ships. Napoleon would always fire this artillery at enemy camps. Now that Smith had hold of it, he raised the artillery to the walls of the citadel. Thus, the French would find themselves under attack from their own guns!

Soon after their arrival in Acre, the French soldiers strove to storm the walls of the citadel no less than six times. However, every furious effort ended in failure. Therefore, on March 28, they dug three concentric rows of trenches around the walls and placed their field guns and cannons within them. The innermost trench row led to the city's moat. Napoleon had sent an army officer holding a flag of truce into the enemy camp earlier. The French were not offering a truce, but demanding surrender. Djezzar simply threw the officer into prison. Therefore, the French began firing at the walls. Nonetheless, their cannons were not able to penetrate the strong fortifications. Both the British and the Ottomans took full advantage of the weakness of the French artillery. It did not help that a Turkish rescue fleet arrived with fresh troops and different types of weapons. Then the Jewish advisor to the governor, Haim Farhi, convinced around

8,000 to 9,000 inhabitants of Acre to do whatever they could to prevent the invaders from entering the town.

Napoleon ordered his cannons to keep up the assault. This time, the French were successful in creating a breach in the middle of the eastern wall. However, General Lannes and his men ran against a secret, second line of defenses set up along the eastern section of the Citadel. There was a dry moat, which the French found impossible to scale. Their scaling ladders were too short for the task. The men had to retreat under heavy fire from the enemy forces and the French Army suffered heavy losses.

Over the next few days, the French discovered that they were running short of ammunition. Therefore, Napoleon offered rewards for finding cannonballs. His opponent, Djezzar, decided to offer bounties on enemy heads. March turned into April, and yet, the French did not stop their assault on the walls. Initially, a British sortie managed to halt the French in their tracks. However, they returned soon and drove a mine under the tower. They blew it on April 24. However, the French had miscalculated badly, for the mine destroyed only the front wall of the lower story. Regardless, the troops entered the citadel through this breach and the enemy forces drove them back. Another mine under the same Cursed Tower, as they called it, caused it to collapse partially. The British and the Ottomans pelted the French Army with grenades and rocks. They even threw stinkpots at them. Stinkpots refer to powder kegs containing burning mixtures of sulfur and gunpowder. They gave off acrid smoke.

Then, like an answer to a prayer, a package from Egypt arrived towards the end of April. This package contained large-caliber siege guns. It took six days to set up these siege guns in position. Napoleon knew that time was not on his side, for plague had broken out in the ranks of the French Army once more. Every day, he lost more men. Additionally, he received information about the Ottomans from Cyprus closing in. However, much to Napoleon's relief, his guns sufficed to create the much-needed breach in the walls of the citadel.

Meanwhile, Captain Smith informed the British admiralty that he was expecting certain defeat at the hands of the French. His words seemed prophetic, as the French guns began to boom on May 7. This was because Napoleon had noticed the ships carrying the Ottoman Army from Cyprus, traveling towards them. However, the British admiralty wasted no time either. It sent over ships with supplies and reinforcements. The impatient Napoleon increased the bombardment of the walls, resulting in the French Army entering the second story of the Cursed Tower. The next morning, the daring Captain Smith decided to retaliate. He managed to get back the breach with the help of a group of marines. He held onto his position tenaciously, until more reinforcements arrived, to make the victory complete. When Djezzar witnessed the courage of the naval officer, he was ashamed. He ordered the Ottomans to stand up with courage and fight with gusto!

Napoleon retaliated by spreading propaganda. He requested the printing of two sets of pamphlets, one aimed at the Muslims and the other at Christians. The Muslim pamphlet suggested that Napoleon had already destroyed the pope's power in Rome, as well as the power of the Knights of St. John in Malta. Therefore, the people could view him as the true defender of Islam. The Christian pamphlet suggested that he was a natural successor to the great men renowned as the Crusaders. This indicated that he was a staunch devotee of the Christian faith. However, Captain Smith managed to get a hold of these pamphlets before they could reach the intended recipients. He ordered that the wrong pamphlets reach the wrong factions. Naturally, local goodwill dried up soon!

Then the naval officer had some new leaflets made, specifically for the soldiers in the French Army. Every leaflet that reached a soldier's trench suggested the sultan would offer free and safe passage out of Syria for anyone wishing to surrender. Irked beyond measure, Napoleon wrote that Captain Smith was a crazy young man. The captain did not mind! Instead, he relaxed and let the propaganda war take a deep hold on the mindsets of both the French Army and the local populace. After all, the citadel had sufficient reinforcements and supplies.

Nonetheless, Napoleon was not about to give up. He would launch another assault on May 10, even with the sweltering Middle Eastern sun beating down upon the heads of his soldiers. In fact, Napoleon himself wished to take over the command. However, General Kleber persuaded him not to, and took over the job himself. Captain Smith, as usual, was in charge of the defense. The assault failed, and the French experienced a chilling defeat. General Kleber could do nothing, except order his men to retreat. To top it all off, Captain Smith penned a rather cheeky letter to Brigadier General Napoleon. He informed Napoleon that he had been aware of all the efforts that the French commander had been making over the past few days to raise the siege. He also appreciated the preparations that Napoleon had made to care for the wounded and to leave not a single Frenchman behind him. Having said this, the naval officer resorted to taunting, wherein he reminded Napoleon about the instability of human affairs. The letter ended with the warning that not all of Asia was waiting to add to Napoleon's glory, and he had better always keep that in mind.

Napoleon knew when he was beaten. He decided to cut his losses on May 20 and return to Egypt. His troops were ill and exhausted. Over a third of the French Army was disabled or dead. He buried his dream of establishing a French Empire forever.

The Battles

While Napoleon was busy with his Siege of Acre, the Ottomans at Damascus were busy raising a huge army. The intention was to relieve the men fighting at the Citadel of Acre. Towards this end, Achmed Bey managed to put together a force comprising anywhere between 25,000 to 35,000 men. Napoleon knew of the approach of this army. Therefore, he sent General Kleber, with around 2,000 soldiers under his command, to intercept the Ottomans. This was the French Army of the Orient. General Kleber set off, under the cover of darkness, hoping to launch a surprise attack on the unsuspecting Ottomans in the morning. However, he miscalculated with regard to the movements of the army, chancing upon the opponents only after sunrise, at Mount Tabor.

When Kleber sighted the Ottoman Army, he knew that the French were heavily outnumbered. Yet April 16, 1799, would be a day to remember! Kleber divided his men into two small infantry squares. The men fought valiantly, even against repeated cavalry attacks. They were able to repel every attack successfully. However, the men were unable to break ranks, or even move from their positions. They could see water close by but were unable to reach it. Their chance for a complete victory was heading towards a stalemate, albeit temporarily. Fortunately for them, Napoleon was not about to leave his small army to fight on its own. He arrived with reinforcements of another 2,000 men, at around 4:00 p.m. This time, he had his cannons with him. A few shots at the Ottomans sufficed to create complete disarray. By the time the Ottoman Army fled to safety, it had lost around 5,000 soldiers. The French lost only about 300 men. Thus, Napoleon and Kleber inflicted a crushing defeat on Damascus' Army.

General Andre Massena was the commander-in-chief of the French Army in Switzerland. At the First Battle of Zurich, fought between June 4 and 6, 1799, his forces had suffered a resounding defeat at the hands of an angry Austrian Army. The victory emboldened Archduke Charles to think of pushing the French Army out of Switzerland completely. Towards this end, he continued to consolidate his position in Zurich, as well as keeping the fortress of Zurich well supplied. These actions continued throughout the summer. By the time, August came around, the Austrians and Russians were ready to tackle the French once again. In fact, Charles began an assault across the Lippert River, but it failed because the bridges were old and unstable. Before he could plan further, his government decided to send the Archduke to the Netherlands. As a result, General Alexander Korsakov and Baron Hotze had to take charge of the Russian and Austrian Armies. Both did not have much experience. Therefore, they hoped that Field Marshal Suvarov of Russia would join them soon. He was highly experienced and a legendary war figure. While waiting for his forces to arrive, they decided to divide the area into two sections, one for the Russian forces, and the other for the Austrian forces.

While all this was going on, General Massena was putting up all manner of fortifications to tackle the enemy forces. Due to the arrival of reinforcements, his army now numbered 75,000 men. He sent a small group of men to tackle Suvarov's forces, who were making their way through the alpine passes. Then, he focused on the Russian Army under the command of Korsakov. While a section of his army would attack the central column of the Russians, another section would ensure that Hotze's forces could never come to the former's aid at all. At the same time, he had a surprise up his sleeve! He had kept one part of his army to cross the Limmat River in the night and move directly against Zurich. This would enable the group to get behind the Russians, thereby cutting them off from Zurich.

Massena's forces began the river crossing on the night of September 24-25, 1799. At 6:00 a.m., the men in front went for the Russians guarding the river and the bridges. By 9:00 a.m., the entire French Army was across the river and aiming for the Russian flanks and rear. This was not all. Massena utilized two ruses. One gave the impression that a desperate French Army was heading towards the Russian center. Korsakov thought that this was the French Army's big move and sent across reinforcements as quickly as he could. The newly arrived soldiers pushed the French soldiers back across the Limmat River. As these tactics continued, more and more soldiers found themselves separated from the main Russian Army. The second ruse consisted of heavy activity in front of Russian positions. The Russian commander felt that this was Massena's main attack. He was soon locking himself into positions that he could not move out of and thus the feints sufficed to freeze Korsakov.

With regard to the Austrians, Massena sent a small group of men to swim across the Limmat River, set up a bridgehead and begin a big attack. This was so surprising that, without thinking, Hotze organized his forces and then, taking along his chief of staff, rode onto the road. It was a misty morning, and he did not see the French patrol lying in wait for him. Hotze died with several bullet wounds in him. The news of his sudden death paralyzed the Austrian forces though Hotze had left behind a second-in-command. However, he was so inexperienced that he ordered his men to abandon Switzerland completely. Even Korsakov began to retreat.

General Massena focused on Zurich and Winterhur, with the aim of isolating Korsakov completely. Towards this end, the French began bombarding the fortress. The army succeeded in driving Korsakov out of Switzerland. The general then took the remaining soldiers of his army and raced for the Rhine. While the French suffered just about 1,000 or so casualties, the Austrians suffered 7,000. Around 6,000 men became the prisoners of the French.

And then the Battle of Abu Qir happened in July 1799. Napoleon had left a small garrison of French soldiers at Abu Qir, in order to guard it. The British decided to take advantage of this fact by inviting the Ottomans to launch an attack against the French forces. Accordingly, Mustafa Pasha brought over his Army of Rhodes, comprising around 18,000 soldiers. Accompanying them were Turkish, British and Russian ships. After landing at Abu Qir Bay on July 14, the forces captured the French fort which was located at the tip of the western arm of the Bay. Naturally, Pasha's army found it quite easy to overwhelm the French residing there. Then, the Ottomans dug trenches and waited for reinforcements. They also kept themselves ready to face the French counterattack, which they knew would happen. The Ottomans dug themselves in, in three lines. The imposing Fort of Abu Qir was behind them.

Napoleon quickly gathered an army of 7,700 men, carrying seventeen guns. As soon as Napoleon reached the fort on July 25, 1799, his infantry launched a vicious attack on each line of fortification with the aid of artillery. In numbers, the French were almost equal to each set of Ottoman defenders. These men exhibited greater organization and discipline in their approach to warfare. Above all, they handled their guns much more ably than the enemy did. Thus, the French routed the Ottomans completely, preventing them from recovering Egypt. At the end of it all, the French had 900 casualties on their hands, with 200 men killed outright. As for the Ottoman Army, around 13,000 died, while 2,000 soldiers went missing. The French took 3,000 prisoners, including Mustafa Pasha. The victory made Napoleon feel that if there was general peace all around, the French might yet be able to retain possession of Egypt.

Napoleon decided to leave Egypt. Historians often wonder if Napoleon deserted his army and fled. This is because he did leave Egypt rather furtively, following orders he received from the French Directoire. The Directory had decided that Napoleon must return to France. Therefore, they dispatched a letter along with Admiral Bruix, who managed to evade the British blockade of Brest in March 1799. He entered the Mediterranean region confidently, since he had sufficient troops along with him. However, he did not take advantage of this fact and caused the British a tremendous amount of concern, prior to returning to Brest. He was not even able to get the Directory's orders to Napoleon in Egypt. They fell into the hands of the British.

Captain Smith understood that it would be advantageous for the British if Napoleon were to return to France. Therefore, while conducting negotiations for the exchange of prisoners, he ensured that the new orders reached him. He hoped that while Napoleon was returning to France via the seas, the British could capture him. However, this gamble failed. After returning to Cairo briefly, Napoleon headed towards the Nile Delta on August 22, informing everyone that he was conducting an inspection. As soon as he reached the delta, he went on board *Le Muiron*, Admiral Ganteaume's flagship. This was a novel ship, well designed and quick in movement. Fortunately, for Napoleon, he encountered no British fleets. The only one he saw was Lord Keith's, moored off the coast of Provence.

When Napoleon landed in France on October 9, 1799, with six officers, everyone welcomed him with triumphant cheers, regardless of whatever had happened in Egypt. Soon after his arrival, Talleyrand and Abbe Sieyes decided that a coup must be planned to end the French Directoire. The aim was to overthrow the existing system of governance, which functioned in alignment with the Directory's order. In its place, the trio wished to bring in a consulate. This would allow the ushering in of a despotic government or dictatorship. It was something that Napoleon had always wanted!

On November 9, 1799, Sieyes and his Legislative Council of Ancients decided that the Ancients, as well as the Lower House or Council of Five Hundred, would gather at the palace in Saint-Cloud, purportedly to shelter from a Jacobin plot rumored to be afoot in Paris. The real reason was ensuring that the councils remained under the intimidation of Napoleon's troops at a location that was far away from the city.

On November 10, 1799, when both councils gathered at the palace in Saint Cloud, Napoleon fumbled and mumbled while making a speech in front of the Ancients. He received plenty of abuse for his actions. However, the Council of Five Hundred, which noticed the presence of troops all around, understood that something nasty was brewing. Napoleon ran away from the hall of the Council of Five Hundred. However, Lucien Bonaparte, Sieyes and Joachim Murat took charge of the situation. They sent in grenadiers, who formally dissolved the Council of Five Hundred. The grenadiers also forced the Ancients to decree the collapse of the French Directoire. The councils cooperated. They dictated the start of a new consular government with Napoleon as France's First Consul. His assistant consuls would be Roger Duclos and Sieyes. By November 14, 1799, Napoleon set up residence at the Luxembourg Palace.

Egypt after Napoleon

Unlike what Napoleon had imagined, the Egyptians did not view the French as liberators, even though the French remained in their country for another two years.

After Napoleon left, General Kleber took control. His first step was to arrange for the evacuation of the French troops. The French government wanted its army back home as quickly as possible, since the developments in Europe were rather worrisome for them. Therefore, Kleber initiated negotiations with the Ottoman Empire in September 1799. However, he outlined rather ambitious terms. To begin with, he wanted the end of the Second Coalition. Then, the Ottomans were to return the Ionian Islands to the French, as well as end their Siege of Malta. The Ottomans retaliated by seizing the border post of al 'Arish on December 29. Meanwhile, the French Army was becoming increasingly mutinous. Kleber gave his consent to the Convention of al 'Arish on January 24, 1800. The Ottomans agreed to help the French Army return to France safely, and even paid for the redeployment. However, they would not give up the Ionian Islands or drop out of the Second Coalition.

While the Ottomans were happy at the way things were progressing, the British were not. They did not want an experienced French Army returning to France. However, France agreed to confirm the convention. Unfortunately, communications were slow and tedious! In March 1800, Admiral Lord Keith, the British commander-in-chief for the Mediterranean region, declared that he was not ready to accept the terms outlined in the convention. By this time, the French Army had withdrawn to Cairo where an army of 40,000 Ottomans waited.

Next came the Battle of Heliopolis. At this time, General Kleber was in charge of the French Army in Egypt. Kleber was striving to negotiate with both the Ottomans and the British, seeking their assistance in evacuating the remaining members of his army from the country. European Operations required their presence. Towards this end, he had even signed an accord titled "The Convention of El Arich" on January 23, 1800. However, a dithering sultan and the presence of internal dissentions within the British Army prevented the implementation of the accord. In fact, Admiral Keith refused to respect the accord. He wanted Kleber and his army to surrender. Both the British and the Ottomans believed that Kleber's forces were too weak to fight their combined armies. The sultan called upon the people of Cairo to rise up and fight the invaders.

An extremely confident Ibrahim Bey, commanding an army of 40,000 soldiers, confronted the French Army of the Orient with its 10,000 men at the ancient site of Heliopolis, just outside Cairo. Kleber decided to launch a surprise attack at dawn on March 20, 1800. The strategy was a huge success, for only a fraction of the huge Ottoman army put up some kind of resistance. While the French lost around 300 men, the Ottomans lost 6,000 men and nineteen guns. Thus, the French were able to tackle the immediate threat to their security with aplomb. They retook Cairo and suppressed revolts initiated by the local population. As a result, the Ottomans no longer seemed dangerous. France could continue to control Egypt without fearing them.

On April 20, 1800, the general and his forces found themselves pushed into the Port of Genoa in Italy by the advancing Austrian forces. As if this was not enough, Massena's men found themselves under attack by a section of the British Royal Navy too, with the distinct possibility that no one would be able to rescue them. Regardless, the group decided that it would defend Genoa to the last man, without flinching. While all this was going on, Napoleon's Army of the Reserve was heading towards Milan, after successfully negotiating the Great St. Bernard Pass in the Swiss Alps. After taking Milan, Napoleon's army was issuing threats to the main Austrian Army. This prompted Peter Ott, the Austrian general, to begin the siege at Genoa. It continued for almost sixty days. During this time, the plague hit the citizens of Genoa. Furthermore, the civilian populace was in revolt, for they wanted the besieged French forces to capitulate. They were against the idea of negotiations for exchanging prisoners.

Finally, when just a day's rations remained on June 4, Massena's negotiator decided to evacuate the French Army from Genoa. Massena's men had already attempted a few breakout sorties, knowing that reinforcements were about to arrive. Regardless, the general had to come to the negotiating table if his men were to survive. He would surrender the city, if his men could leave with full honors. They should be able to reach French-controlled territory safely. While some of the men left by sea, the majority of Massena's army marched out of the city. Although starving and exhausted, the troops gathered their equipment and marched on the road along the coastline, in order to reach France. Napoleon could not find enough words of praise for the courage, tenacity, daring and ingenuity of Massena and his troops.

Located on the Upper Rhine, Stockach proved to be a major communication center for the Austrian forces during the Revolutionary Wars. In fact, the Austrian Army tended to look upon this place as its headquarters. While Lake Constance lay just a few kilometers away from Stockach, the upper Danube flowed 20-25 kilometers north of it.

Due to its strong presence in Switzerland, the French Army was able to cross the Rhine at Schaffhuasen and flank the main Austrian Army settled in the fortress at Hohenweil. The opponents quickly surrendered. Meanwhile, on May 3, 1800, General Moreau's French forces and General Kray's Austrian forces battled it out at Engen in the Battle of Stockach on May 3, 1800. At the same time, 28,000 men, belonging to the French Right-Wing Corps and under the command of General LeCourbe, confronted 9,000 soldiers of the Austrian Army under the leadership of Prince Joseph of

Lorraine. Although each side lost almost 2,000 men, the French emerged victorious. When General Kray heard about the loss at Stockach, he ordered his forces to retreat all the way to the fortifications present at Ulm. Apart from causing a huge disturbance to the position of the Austrian forces, the Battle of Stockach caused considerable losses of stored supplies.

Napoleon was well aware that he had to thank General Massena for enabling the Army of the Reserve to cross the Swiss Alps. The general had forced the Austrians to attack him at Genoa, thereby giving Napoleon and his men sufficient time to move through the pass, take the Austrians by surprise and ultimately, defeat General Michael von Melas' army. Napoleon expressed his delight and trust in Massena by offering him a commander's post in the First Army of the Republic or the Italian Army.

The Battle of Montebello was fought on June 9, 1800, between France and Austria. While General Lannes had 8,000 men in his Advance Guard of the French Army of the Reserve, General Ott of Austria had 18,000 men under his command. The Austrians also possessed thirty-five guns.

To begin with, both parties commenced maneuvering their forces, albeit in total confusion. Neither knew where the opponent actually was and they met each other by accident! When Lannes and his men finished crossing the River Po and began moving westwards between its southern bank and the Appennines, they encountered Ott's forces. The French were heading towards Voghera, while Ott's men had positioned themselves at Casteggio. During the initial stages of the battle, Lannes' forces had to retreat. Soon enough, General Victor appeared at the scene, along with his corps of 5,000 soldiers. The Austrians had to flee. The French pursued them through Montebello. This made the Austrians determined to be more cautious in future. They could not afford to be aggressive against the French, if they were to take them on at Alessandria. The French lost around 500 men at the Battle of Montebello, while the Austrian losses amounted to 4,000 soldiers.

Napoleon was in pursuit of an evasive Austrian Army, keen on regaining its secure supply lines. Towards this end, the army was either going towards the east, by passing north of the River Po, or moving towards Genoa and the Royal Navy in the south. On June 13, he spied the main Austrian forces at Alessandria. The Bromida River and the plain attached to it lay between both the forces. Thinking quickly, Napoleon dispatched a division to the north and another one to the south, in order to prevent the Austrian Army from escaping. This reduced the strength of his main army to almost half of the strength of the Austrian forces. The gleeful Austrians launched an attack immediately on June 14, 1800. This was the Battle of Marengo and it happened on the same day General Kleber was assassinated by an enemy in the guise of a beggar who stabbed him to death as the general extended his hand in greeting. By 11:00 a.m., the Austrians had forced the French forces back along their entire line. Napoleon realized that the line might break. He sent hurried messages to the forces traveling north and south, requesting their return. At the same time, he urged the Reserve Army, which was the Guard and Monnier's Division, to move forward. It helped that the Austrians paused at midday, to regroup.

At 1:00 p.m., the Austrians resumed the battle. General Ott's forces strove to cut off the line of retreat for the forces in the center, as well as to turn the French right. It appeared as if the majority of Napoleon's forces would suffer annihilation. Therefore, instead of focusing on the crumbling forces in the center, Napoleon sent his reserve soldiers to confront Ott on the right. For some time, there was relief. However, by 3:00 p.m., the French forces found themselves having to retreat along their line once again, on the brink of defeat. At this point, Austrian Commander-in-Chief Melas decided to retire from the battlefield and have his subordinate, General Zach, take charge. At the same time, General Desaix reached the spot with Boudet's Division, returning from the south. While Zach took until 4:30 p.m. to gather his troops together, the retreating French forces rallied themselves to battle the Austrians once again.

General Desaix deployed Boudet's Division along the road from where the Austrians would pursue them. Thus, the central Austrian column pursuing the retreating French walked into an unexpected ambush. Now in complete disarray, they fled. The flanking forces found themselves without any support. Unfortunately, General Desaix lost his life in the act of turning a sure defeat into a glorious victory. While the French lost around 7,000 men, the Austrians lost around 6,000 soldiers. They also lost forty guns. The French took 8,000 Austrians prisoners.

Next it was the Austrian Army of the Upper Rhine which decided to engage the French Army of the Rhine in battle at Hochstadt on June 19, 1800. General (FZM) Kray was the man in charge of the Austrian forces numbering around 70,000. However, it was General (FZM) Sztarray, with his 16,000 men who actually engaged in battle against 25,000 French soldiers, under the overall command of General Moreau. These soldiers were the right-wing corps, functioning under the leadership of General Lecourbe.

The Austrians were surprised when General Lecourbe's men managed to cross the Danube River near Hochstadt and surrounded them. Although the Austrians fought long and hard, they could not defeat the French. Once again, France took charge of both sides of the river, thereby severing supply lines to the Austrian forces. No one knows how many French casualties there were, but the Austrians lost close to 1,000 men. Several thousand became the prisoners of the French. General Kray had no choice but to give up Ulm, as well as most of Bavaria.

As mentioned earlier, the French Army had taken over Malta while facing very little opposition because the French had promised to protect and respect the locals' freedom of worship, as well as their religious privileges. This was in alignment with the Articles of Capitulation of Quebec, signed on board L'Orient on September 18, 1759, during the Seven Years' War. Representatives of both the British and French Crowns had been present then. Yet, under the new French administrator, Regnaud de St. Jean d'Angely, who was placed in charge of French-controlled Malta, the Articles of Capitulation became relegated to the background. Many locals lost their pensions. Creditors did not have the permission to recover their dues. These actions were a direct hit on their livelihood. Then the French tried to suppress religious institutions.

Additionally, they grabbed the silver and gold relics in reliquaries, for converting into bullion to fund the French Army. As a result, although the Knights and Maltese forces had initially given in rather tamely to the French, the local inhabitants decided that they were not willing to accept French domination so easily after all. They strongly rebelled and were eventually assisted by the British Navy in their quest for independence, culminating in one last battle against the French on September 5, 1800.

Thus, Malta was extremely grateful to the British Navy and decided that it would like to be part of the British Empire. Towards this end, locals offered their island as a present to Sir Alexander Ball, along with the Maltese Declaration of Rights. According to this declaration, Malta would henceforth be under the protection of the British Empire though the king or queen would have no right to hand over the Maltese Islands to any other power. The island, along with Minorca, became the launching pad for British naval expeditions such as various forays into Egypt in 1801 and the Ionian Islands between 1809 and 1814. Malta was also the trade center for goods coming in from the Orient, thereby providing a source of contraband against the continental system. The Treaty of Paris of May 30, 1814, ensured that Malta remained under British control for some time.

The Battle of Hohenlinden, fought on December 5, 1800, proved to be the decisive factor in ensuring the collapse of the Second Coalition. The battle took place about 30km to the east of Munich in Germany, near the Inn Valley. Archduke John believed that his Austrian Army of the Upper Rhine could tackle the French easily, since they seemed to be in retreat. Therefore, he divided his 130,000-strong army into multiple columns. In contrast, the French Army of the Rhine, under the leadership of General Moreau, was comprised of just about 100,000 soldiers. Nonetheless, neither group found the going easy, since it was winter and snowing all the time. The archduke's columns could not move rapidly enough to reach the French Army. The flanking columns suffered the most. Additionally, none of the columns found it easy to keep in communication with one another. In fact, the left-wing column lost its way completely. Thus, it became something of a problem when the archduke's central column engaged with the French central column under the leadership of General Ney. At the same time, General Richepanse, who was in charge of a group, urged his men to attack the Austrian columns on the rear and flanks. The assaults from all sides sufficed to fragment the Austrian Army completely. Thus, without any preparation or planning, the French Army gained an unexpected victory. While French casualties numbered 5,000, Austrian casualties numbered 18,000.

This battle ended the campaign against Austria in Germany. Above all, General Moreau conducted himself so marvelously that his reputation reached France before he did. Later on, Napoleon would find this to be something of a political problem!

Treaty of Luneville (February 9, 1801)

After Austria was defeated at both the Battle of Marengo and the Battle of Hohenlinden, an agreement was signed on February 9, 1801, between the Holy Roman Emperor, Francis II, and the representatives of the French Republic. Francis II stood as the representative of the Habsburg Monarchy and all the other rulers who governed over various territories in the Holy Roman Empire. The officials who affixed their signatures to the document were Count Ludwig von Cobenzl on the Austrian side and Joseph Bonaparte on the French side. The former was the foreign minister of Austria.

According to this treaty, there would always be amity, good understanding and peace amongst all the parties concerned, forever. Austria had to give up certain holdings that lay within the boundaries of the Holy Roman Empire. In turn, the French took over everything on the left bank of the Rhine but relinquished any claim on the territories lying east of the river. The parties also settled the boundaries with regard to any contested areas in Italy. Similarly, while France gained access to the Grand Duchy of Tuscany, Ferdinand III (Grand Duke of Tuscany) gained access to territorial compensations in Germany. Both the parties agreed to respect the independence of specific republics.

This treaty, along with the Treaty of Amiens that came into being in 1802, was sufficient to end the Second Coalition. Russia had already left towards the end of 1799, becoming increasingly anti-British in the bargain. Therefore, Britain had to go it alone. Nonetheless, France could never remain peaceful or friendly with other nations for long. It was back at war with Austria in 1805.

As of 1801, the world referred to Egypt as the master key to reach every trading nation on earth, given that it was the shortest route for transporting goods back and forth from the east and west. However, if the French remained in possession of Egypt, this route posed a great danger for Great Britain. It would allow the French to use it as a staging post for invading India, which was under British control at that time. Therefore, it was imperative to expel the French from Egypt. This led to the Second Battle of Abu Qir.

At the time, the French Army of the Orient was just about 10,000 men strong. General Menou was in command of the forces. With regard to the British, they had a 20,000-strong army which was active in the field at that time. This army would be part of a three-pronged attack on the French. Lord Abercrombie's men, with the support of a smaller Ottoman Army, would position themselves along the Egyptian coast. The grand vizier would lead a larger Ottoman Army through Palestine and attack the enemy. The third line of attack would come from a combined army of men belonging to Britain and India. These troops would land on the coast of the Red Sea. From there, they would march alongside the Nile River and reach Cairo.

Due to bad weather conditions, General Abercrombie could not reach the designated spot on time. However, his forces, led by General Moore, reached Abu Qir Bay on March 8, 1801. His absence gave the French sufficient time to organize an attack. Around 4,000 French troops engaged in a stiff battle on March 13, which led to the establishment of a beachhead. The French managed to force the British towards a defensive position around 5km from Alexandria. Menou, who had been placed in charge of the French forces after General Kleber's June 14, 1800, assassination, marched towards Alexandria. By March 18, the British had even taken over the Castle of Abu Qir. The French field army reached Alexandria on March 19. Menou launched a surprise attack in the darkness of night, on March 20. However, General Moore managed to hold off the main French attacks.

The next morning, on March 21, the French Army launched another surprise attack on the British forces. The British were expecting it but had misjudged both the direction and timing of the French attack.ABO Fortunately, reinforcements arrived just in time, enabling them to renew their artillery fire. In fact, the British inflicted heavy casualties on the French Army. The French lost around 3,000 men. At the same time, around 1,400 British soldiers either received wounds or died. The greatest loss came in the wounding of General Abercrombie. A musket ball injured his thigh so grievously that the general died just a week later.

When the Ottoman Army arrived to join the main British Army towards the end of April, it marched towards Cairo and laid siege to the city on June 21. There were 13,000 French forces hiding in the garrison there. However, they capitulated on June 27. Meanwhile, the combined forces of India and Great Britain had made their landing on the coast of the Red Sea in early June. They began their crossing of the Egyptian desert on June 19. Nonetheless, they had no opportunity to play a direct role in the battle. Even France's new Mamluk allies stayed away.

General Menou and his troops found themselves trapped in Alexandria, for the British had followed them there. General Hutchinson had taken over from General Abercrombie. The French surrendered on August 30. Two weeks later, Menou's men departed for France. Menou, himself, decided to remain in Egypt. He converted to Islam and married an Egyptian woman.

Assassination of Tsar Paul (March 23, 1801)

Tsar Paul I, son of Catherine the Great, was an unpopular ruler. Obsessed with the Prussian Arm, he made it compulsory for soldiers to demonstrate their drills in front of his Mikhailovsky Palace in St. Petersburg, at 11:00 a.m., every single day. These elite guards did not relish taking part in the monarch's charades. The tsar went all out to provide relief for serfs, albeit at the heavy expense of landowners. He appointed bureaucrats to look after state and central governances and believed that his people would be contaminated by the ideologies of the French Revolution. Therefore, he refused to let his subjects travel abroad. He refused to let foreign books or periodicals enter the country and it was obvious that he had no idea of how to formulate foreign policies. As if this was not enough, the tsar often gave in to outbursts of uncontrollable rage and bouts of capriciousness. People doubted his sanity.

Monday, March 23, 1801, was a cold day. That night, the tsar hosted a grand dinner party at his St. Petersburg palace. His son, Grand Duke Alexander, was one of the guests. Once the party was over, the tsar retired to his private chambers. According to historical accounts, around 1:00 a.m. someone opened one of the palace doors to admit a group of drunken conspirators, led by General Leo Bennigsen and Count von Pahlen. The latter was the military commander of St. Petersburg. While von Pahlen made his way to Alexander's rooms, Bennigsen led his guard officers to the tsar's chambers. Once there, they managed to overpower the valets on duty and broke down the door leading to Paul's bedroom. However, the tsar had heard them coming and had taken cover behind a screen. Unfortunately, Bennigsen and his group found him, for they became suspicious when they found the bedclothes still warm. They battered the tsar and throttled him with a scarf.

Their actions were in direct contrast to what the conspirators had decided earlier. They had an abdication document ready for the signature of the tsar. However, they changed their mind when von Pahlen stated that when someone wished to make an omelet, one had to break the eggs first. It followed that Alexander I would take over as the new tsar. However, although he was not party to what had taken place, he could not help nurturing a guilty conscience for the rest of his life.

Although the Brits and the Danes were not at war in the formal sense, the British were keen to prevent Denmark and Sweden from becoming allies of the French. Therefore, the British Navy set sail for the northern point of Jutland on March 18. Despite the whirling snow, they sailed to Kattegat. Once there, the British sent an ultimatum to Copenhagen. However, the Danes rejected it. Vice-Vice-Admiral Nelson had a bold plan for attacking the Danes. His fleet and higher authorities accepted it. Therefore, when the wind was fair on March 30, the British fleet of fifty-two ships, whose towering sails gleamed in the sun, moved between the narrow gap present between Sweden and Denmark. After crossing the gap, the ships laid anchor about five miles from Copenhagen and successfully survived a harmless cannonade from batteries stationed at Elsinore on the Danish bank.

Along with Admiral Parker and other senior officers, Vice-Vice-Admiral Nelson boarded a schooner, in order to make a keen survey of the defenses surrounding the city. The harbor had natural protection in the form of shoals. The Trekroner Fort had a supply of seventy or more heavy guns in place along with nineteen warships, with their masts down. They stood in a line, one and a half miles long. After the survey, the group spent hours roaming about in small boats, discussing strategies for attacking the weakest point of the

Danish defenses at the southeastern end of the city. How should they place the buoys such that they would guide the ships through the difficult and narrow channel to begin an attack? A conference took place on Parker's flagship, the *London*, on March 31. After this, they completed placing positioning the buoys. Nelson's spirits were so high that he treated his captains to dinner on April 1, on the *Elephant*.

The wind was fair again the next morning. However, the pilots of a few ships refused to lead the way through the channel, believing it to be extremely dangerous. Finally, the person commanding the *Bellona*, a veteran of the Nile, volunteered. At 9:30 a.m. on April 2, twelve ships, as well as some frigates and bomb ketches, began moving through the channel, marking the beginning of the Battle of Copenhagen. The Danish guns gave them a rough time, even causing three ships to run aground on the shoals. However, the British seafarers remained levelheaded. This helped the rest of the squadron to anchor at their destination in a line. All the ships brought their broadsides to rear. Once in position, the British guns began to retaliate, aiming at the moored Danish ships. The attack progressed with clinical precision, wherein every gun fired a broadside from a range of 200 yards, once every forty seconds. The Danes remained tenacious and energetic in their reply to this assault. The sound and smoke attracted crowds of citizens, who watched the progress of the battle by climbing onto church towers and rooftops.

The stiff resistance of the Danes caused Admiral Hyde Parker to send a signal, ordering the British ships to retreat. However, Vice-Admiral Nelson decided that he would pretend not to see the signal. This was a terrible act of insubordination on the part of the second-in-command of the British Fleet, but Nelson did not care. In fact, he was enjoying himself! A cannonball caused splinters to fly off the seventy-four-gun battleship, the *Elephant's* main mast, around 1:30 p.m. Nelson coolly stated that even though it was warm work, he would not be elsewhere even if someone were to pay him a thousand pounds. Some years ago, during the Siege of Calvi, the Vice-Admiral had lost sight in his right eye. Therefore, he placed his spyglass against this blind eye and, turning to the captain of the *Elephant*, Thomas Foley, stated that since he had just one eye, he had the right to be blind at times. He also told Foley that he could not see any signal suggesting that the British disengage from the ongoing battle. He was not to know that Admiral Parker had not really expected Nelson to follow his orders, especially when the latter had decided that it was not correct to quit an about-to-win scenario!

Around 3:00 p.m., the Danes decided that they could fight no more. The carnage was horrific to witness! Many of their ships suffered raging fires, and the Danish flagship simply blew up. As a result, many of the remaining ships decided to strike their colors. When the two leading ships of Admiral Parker arrived on the scene, more ships decided to surrender. The Danish commander readily accepted the truce that Vice-Admiral Nelson offered. Thus, everything was over by 4:00 p.m. While British casualties numbered around 1,000, Danish casualties were much higher. The next day, on Good Friday, Crown Prince Frederick of Denmark invited Vice-Admiral Nelson to a state dinner. When he stepped ashore, the people of Copenhagen greeted him with a mixture of displeasure, admiration and curiosity. At the dinner table, Nelson praised the Danes for their pluck. They had resisted courageously for four hours. This impressed everyone, leading to the signing of an armistice on April 9, 1801.

Napoleon Treaties

The French Revolution had led to a deep misunderstanding between the clerical and papal representatives in both Paris and Rome. This breach was the direct result of church confiscations and reforms that the revolutionaries had enacted at that time. When Napoleon entered the picture as the

First Consul, he decided to link up with these representatives in order to redefine the status of the Roman Catholic Church in France. As a result, the group reached a formal agreement on July 15, 1801. This was the Concordat, which they made public on Easter 1802.

As per the Concordat, Napoleon would have the right to nominate bishops of his choice. He ensured the redistribution of parishes and bishoprics and also granted permission for the establishment of seminaries. In turn, Pope Pius VII decided to condone the actions of all those who had made away with church property. The French government would compensate for the loss of these properties via suitable salaries for curates and bishops. Finally, some unilateral provisions were added to the agreement by the French government. These articles organized the structure of Catholic Church, as well as the religions of Jews and Protestants. The articles also focused on the remuneration that the state had to provide for the clergy. It was essential for the state to look after the allocation and funding related to diverse places of worship, as well as the representatives of these religious communities.

With Napoleon in the seat of First Consul of France, the British felt that its relationship with France was not progressing well at all. In fact, the entire nation of Great Britain was sick of warfare between the

English and the French. Therefore, when Henry Addington took over as the new premier of Britain, after the fall of Prime Minister William Pitt the Younger's government in 1801, he decided to put an end to all these continental entanglements. He wanted to make peace and preserve it, and hoped that France wished for the same. Accordingly, Addington set up secret talks in London in 1801. Throughout the summer, Britain's foreign secretary, Lord Hawkesbury, and the French diplomat, Monsieur Otto, had talks with one another. Soon, they affixed their respective signatures to a preliminary agreement at the beginning of October. France would benefit most through this deal. While the papal states and two Sicilies would be returned to their former rulers, France would retain control over the Savoy, the Netherlands, Piedmont and the West Bank of the Rhine River. Britain would retain control over Ceylon and Trinidad but would let go off various islands in the Caribbean, the Cape of Good Hope, Egypt and Malta.

William Pitt the Younger approved of this agreement too. The former governor-general of India, Lord Cornwallis, agreed to take up the role of ambassador-extraordinary, in order to document the final treaty. In the meantime, William Wilberforce, a politician against slavery, had been urging Addington to include the abolition of slavery in the treaty's terms. However, the premier did not wish anything to come in the way of progress of peace, although he did sympathize with the victims of a flourishing slave trade in the continent. Thus, despite not being a diplomat and knowing very little French, Lord Cornwallis set off for an interview with the First Consul at Paris. In November, he reached the Hotel de Ville in Amiens.

Joseph Bonaparte, Napoleon's elder brother, led the French deputation, which included France's foreign minister, Talleyrand. The English representatives liked Joseph but found his habit of offering concessions in private on a single day, and ruling them out in public the next day, extremely trying. As a result, the wrangling over details dragged on for months. An irritated Cornwallis threatened to walk out if the French did not settle matters within the next eight days. As a result, the Peace of Amiens was enacted on March 27, 1802. Unfortunately, the truce did not last for more than a year. Britain and France were back at war once again as of May 1803.

Many people fell for Napoleon's brilliant oratory, which focused on the stability of the French government, moderation, order and justice. Additionally, he had successfully disbanded the Second Coalition. The French populace appreciated the fact that a competent political leader was in charge of the nation's affairs. Therefore, when it was time for a second national referendum, there was hardly any opposition to Napoleon becoming the First Consul for life. The voting took place on August 2, 1802. He received 99.7 percent approval from the public!

On April 12, 1798, 121 representatives in charge of diverse territories/cantons in Switzerland came together to proclaim the birth of a unified Helvetic Republic. They even confirmed the creation of a new constitution. This constitution remained in alignment with the ideologies of the French Revolution, because France was in control at that time.

However, soon after Napoleon's troops left the Republic in July 1802, the Helvetic Republic began to experience unrest all over again. The representatives of the former system in the newly formed republic took every opportunity to attack the new order or central government, beginning August 1, 1802. The majority of the urban populace refused to accept a centralized system of government, citing that it had no link to the traditions of Switzerland. The rural populace had wanted to be allowed membership into the existing political system. They'd wanted liberty and equal rights within the old systems. They had never wanted an entirely new system. Liberty had only two meanings. One was that a person could do whatever he or she wanted. Secondly, liberty meant no one had to pay taxes. It did not help that various nations, including France, dumped thousands and thousands of soldiers in their territory, thereby depriving the civil population of essential resources.

Worried that the happenings in the Helvetic Republic would have a disastrous effect on the whole of Europe, Napoleon stepped in to halt the ongoing civil war and restore peace. He even invited a delegation from the Helvetic Republic to Paris for a conference. In October 1802, the French troops found themselves without a choice. They had to invade the republic, in order to put down the rebels. Realizing that the people of Switzerland would never accept the formation of a centralized state, Napoleon restored the thirteen member states which had been in existence before. He added six more cantons, bringing the total to nineteen. All the cantons had equal rights. France would also later return the three cantons that had been under its control since 1798. Thus, the total number of federalistic structures or cantons would rise to twenty-two, each with its own borders. In order to preserve political equality and equality in laws for all citizens, Napoleon also signed the Act of Mediation on February 19, 1803. The act abolished the Helvetic Republic and restored the original Swiss Confederation. It also signaled the end of five years of French rule.

While canoeing down the Mississippi River, French explorer René-Robert Cavelier de La Salle claimed the territory of Louisiana in the name of King Louis XIV of France. Eighty years later, long after the king had been executed and a new system of government established, France ceded this territory to Spain. It had to give up its other North American holdings to Great Britain, due to being defeated in the French and Indian War. Then, in 1800, Napoleon Bonaparte reclaimed the territory in exchange for placing the Spanish king's son-in-law on the throne of newly-created Etruria in Italy. Napoleon also received six warships. Spain and France agreed upon this via a secret treaty, the Treaty of San Ildefonso. Soon enough, the signing of the treaty became public knowledge, causing the President of the United States, Thomas Jefferson, terrible anxiety.

Ever since 1795, a treaty between the United States and Spain had ensured that American farmers and merchants could use the Mississippi River for transporting goods. They could also store these goods in New Orleans, without having to pay export duties. These agreements would change once Napoleon took over Louisiana. Therefore, the Americans began to debate the idea of going to war with the French. They even kept thousands of men ready to fight at a moment's notice. However, slave rebellions, yellow fever and wintry conditions proved to be heavy obstacles in the implementation of their plans. Therefore, Jefferson gave up the idea of going to war with the French. Instead, he requested that Napoleon sell him certain territories. Towards this end, he even sent two special negotiators, Minister Robert Livingston and Special Envoy James Monroe, to France. The U.S. was ready to pay $9.375 million for the purchase of Florida and New Orleans. Livingston argued that they should ask for two-thirds of Louisiana, just north of the Arkansas River. This territory would be an apt buffer between British Canada and French Louisiana.

Luckily, the Americans did not have to negotiate much. Napoleon himself suggested that he would sell Louisiana to the Americans for $11.25 million, on April 11, 1803. Additionally, the Americans would forgive France's $3.75 million debt. Napoleon wanted the money immediately, since he needed funds for fighting the British. Therefore, the United States borrowed money from two European banks, at an interest rate of six percent, and completed the purchase on April 30, 1803. However, not until 1823 was it able to repay the loan!

According to the 1802 Treaty of Amiens, France had agreed to stop meddling in the internal affairs of other countries. However, Napoleon engaged in changing the international system in Germany, the

Netherlands, Italy and Switzerland. He insisted that Great Britain would have no voice in the handling of European affairs. Even Russia felt that Napoleon was not keen on a peaceful resolution of France's differences with diverse European powers. It did not help that Great Britain began to lose markets and control over its territories. In fact, it began to fear that Napoleon would start threatening its overseas colonies. Therefore, the country no longer felt obliged to honor the Treaty of Amiens. On May 18, 1803, Britain declared war against France. In turn, Napoleon began to prepare for an invasion of Great Britain. France also invaded neutral Hanover and captured it on June 1, 1803. Napoleon had it incorporated into the Confederation of the Rhine too.

Louis-Antoine-Henri de Bourbon-Conde, Duke d'Enghien, was a French prince. When the French Revolution broke out, the prince emigrated, along with his father. He joined his grandfather's émigré army in 1792, until the army dissolved after the Treaty of Luneville in 1801. After a secret marriage to Charlotte de Rohan-Rochefort, he settled down at Ettenheim in Baden. All was well until 1804. Then, Napoleon received news from his spies that the Duke d'Enghien was involved in a group conspiracy to topple him from his throne. Without bothering to check whether the report was false or true, Napoleon ordered the duke's sudden and secret arrest. The French gendarmes brought the prince over to the Castle of Vincennes, near Paris. A hurried court martial sufficed as a trial. A week later, he was executed by firing squad on March 21, 1804. With the last prince of the House of Conde gone, there could be no reconciliation between Napoleon and the Royals. However, even the public was aroused to deep anger over the First Consul's atrocious act.

Prior to the French Revolution, France's legal system was highly confusing. For instance, the south of France followed Roman law, while the north of France followed a system founded on Teutonic Customary law. Both these systems were fundamentally different from one another. Then again, every province and every town had its own legal system, even if the laws proved to be completely irrational at times. No one could protest, since France adhered to the monarchical system of governance. When he became First Consul, Napoleon decided that feudal laws had to go. They were not only confusing, but contradictory in nature. Therefore, he created a commission of four noteworthy jurists to draft a unified and logical legal system. This system was in written format and accessible to all. Thus, the Civil Code of France came into effect on March 21, 1804. This Napoleonic Code served to influence various parts of the world then, and even today.

Napoleon began using his influence and power to place all his supporters in influential positions in the government. Therefore, by 1804, he had a group of people under his control who were loyal to him and him alone. An assassination attempt, and Napoleon's near-death experiences in battles, served to cause his supporters immense worry. Unless his government acquired the status of heredity, they would never be able to put an heir who thought and behaved just like his father on France's throne. As a result, Napoleon's senate decided to crown him Emperor of France and make his family hereditary heirs. On May 18, 1804, the senate held a referendum, which they worded with care. In case, Napoleon had no children of his own, he could adopt an heir. Alternatively, another Bonaparte could occupy the throne. The senate took care to "manage" the vote, such that it looked wonderfully convincing on paper. For instance, while 3.5 million agreed with the decision, only 2,500 people were against it!

Pope Plus VII placed the official crown on Napoleon's head on December 2, 1804, at Notre Dame Cathedral, Paris. Napoleon was now Napoleon I. Josephine became the Empress of France. Over the next few years, Napoleon ensured that his word prevailed always, even while the senate and council of state became mere puppets in his hands.

The Senatus-Consulte awarded the title of "Marshal of the Empire" to the new French emperor on May 19, 1804. This title denoted a grand officer of the first French Empire who possessed a high standing at court. In fact, the creation of the marshalate sufficed to resurrect the abolished title of Marshal of France.

As of 1804, Spain had become an ally of Spain, which angered the British no end. The British government thus ordered a naval squadron to go on the offensive against Spain. This squadron seized three Spanish ships which were transporting treasures from the Americas to Spain. An angered Spain joined France in declaring war against Great Britain on December 14, 1804.

To conclude, the Second Coalition did have some initial successes, thanks to Napoleon's wastage of time and resources in chasing elusive foes. However, soon after he became the Emperor of France, Napoleon wasted no time. He recruited energetic men into the French Army and trained them with vigor and vitality. As a result, a grand army came into being, one so powerful that it was able to crush the next three coalitions with ease.

Formation of the Third Coalition

Napoleon's quest to create a military-controlled empire in Europe alarmed many nations. Furthermore, he left no doubt of his intentions as he made plans to conquer one region after another. He even refused to engage in commercial treaties with Great Britain. This led to the formation of an official third coalition in 1803, comprised of Great Britain, Russia, Prussia, Sweden and a few German provinces. However, the coalition became active only in 1805. It existed from April 11, 1805 to December 1805. Austria agreed to join the Third Coalition on August 9, 1805. Like the other countries who were eternally in danger of attacks from the ambitious Napoleon and his equally ambitious French Army, Austria became determined to lessen the threat.

Napoleon had risen to the top through sheer perseverance and grit. His flamboyant boldness led to the overthrow of the French Directoire and its substitution with a consulate. By assuming the title of Permanent First Consul of France, Napoleon could use his powers to the limit. He also ensured the adoption of the Constitution of the Year VIII and began living at the palace in Tuileries. With the aid of this legitimate Constitution, he hoped to bring in a succession of Bonaparte heirs, such that the earlier Bourbon rulers could never return to power.

Napoleon had also assumed the role of Chief Magistrate of Italy in January 1802. The thirty-member commission of the newly formed Republic of Italy had believed that Napoleon would be perfect for the job of president. He had accepted the post, but refused to reside in Italy. As a result, Francesco Melzi, the vice-president, had taken charge of the day-to-day administrative affairs. However, Napoleon had left an army behind in Italy to ensure that Austria and other European nations did not interfere in the economic and international functioning of this French protectorate. But when France became an empire, and Napoleon, the emperor, it became clear to Italy that it could not proclaim itself a republic any longer. Therefore, on March 17, 1805, just a year after Napoleon's coronation, the Italian Republic became the Kingdom of Italy.

France's hold extended across the Emilia Romagna and Lombardy, not throughout the Italian Peninsula. Regardless, Napoleon decided to take over the kingship of this territory too. On May 26, 1805, he took up the role of King of Italy at a formal ceremony held at the Milan Cathedral. The Iron Crown of the Lombards was the official signature of this kingship. It was a symbol of the Kingdom of

Lombardy, as well as one of the oldest royal insignias of Christendom. The crown highlighted Napoleon's Carolingian credentials.

The Battles

At the beginning of 1805, Napoleon decided that his troops would cross the English Channel and attack Great Britain. Towards this end, he had 2,000 ready ships and a French Grande Armée of 210,000 men. When summer ended, Napoleon's soldiers began their march along the shores of the English Channel. Then, as if he had changed his mind suddenly, Napoleon ordered his stunned soldiers to turn their backs on England! Instead, they would move towards the Rhine. It was obvious that he had heard of the Third Coalition. It was also obvious that he had heard about the Austrians and Russians deciding to join forces to defeat the French Army through sheer numbers. As his army continued to move deeper and deeper into Europe, Napoleon understood that his men would find it difficult to confront the combined might of Russia and Austria. However, there was an advantage too. The forces of both countries were scattered across the continent. They had not yet met. Therefore, if the French Grande Armée moved quickly, it could reach the Austrians before their slow-moving Russian friends did!

The Austrians were confident that Napoleon's main target was Italy. Therefore, General Mack and Archduke Ferdinand set off for the Rhine, taking along 40,000 soldiers with them. These commanders were quite sure that Bavaria would join them in their fight against the French. After all, they could not be very fond of having the French ruling over them! The Austrians stormed into Bavaria on September 10, 1805, without requesting permission, or even reaching any kind of agreement with the Bavarians. Unfortunately for them, Maximilian Joseph, the Elector of Bavaria, decided that he preferred France as an ally. Towards that end, he asked his troops to fall back and just wait for the French allies to arrive. General Mack realized that his men would receive no support from the Bavarians. Therefore, he decided to station his men around Ulm. This way, he would be able to defend the Black Forest, as well as wait for the arrival of the Russian forces in peace. The general was sure that Napoleon's men would cross the Rhine River at Strasbourg and then enter the Black Forest. From there, they would reach the Upper Danube River near Ulm.

Napoleon's troops did cross the Rhine River, but at a place further north. Then, they traveled along the line of the Main and Neckar, until they came upon a section of the Upper Danube River lying between Inglostadt and Dillingen. Napoleon didn't ask the neutral Prussians for permission while moving through their territories; such things had never bothered him! This was a failure on the part of Austrian reconnaissance and intelligence. They had somehow missed the movement of such large troops throughout the area.

Once at the specified place, Napoleon took advantage of the natural terrain, as well as the presence of Marshal Murat's cavalry, to position his troops all around the Austrians. By the time the Austrians woke up to this danger, it was too late. They tried to break through the French positions, but failed completely. Whichever units did manage to escape found themselves so scattered that they could not even communicate with one another. Even the 6,000 cavalrymen led by Archduke Ferdinand, who had fled to safety, found themselves captured within a few weeks. Napoleon demanded that the Austrians give up Ulm. General Mack tried to negotiate, hoping that the Russians would arrive soon. Napoleon agreed to stay put until October 25, knowing that the Russians were far away from the Austrian Army. In case no reinforcements arrived by that point, General Mack could surrender then. However, the general realized the hopelessness of the situation by October 20 and gave up his troops, himself and the city of Ulm.

This was one of Napoleon's greatest successes, and a personal one at that! With barely a shot fired and with just the aid of a strategic maneuver, the French had won the battle. Thus, Ulm was less of a battle, and more of a maneuver and surrender. It boosted French morale to no end and shattered Austrian spirits horrifically!

As we saw earlier, Napoleon was keen to engage the British in battle and this took the form of the Battle of Trafalgar on October 21, 1805. On one side was the British fleet under the command of Vice-Admiral Horatio Nelson, and on the other side was the Franco-Spanish fleet under the joint command of Vice-Admiral Pierre-Charles de Villeneuve and Admiral Don Federico Gravina. While the British squadron was comprised of 27 ships, the Franco-Spanish squadron had 33. The battle began off the western mouth of the Straits of Gibraltar.

Nelson had always been rather daring in his strategies. This time, too, he took a calculated risk, knowing that he had well-trained and highly disciplined troops on his side. Furthermore, even the captains working under him were thoroughly attuned with his ideas and style of warfare. Therefore, he split his fleet into two columns, urging them to storm into the wind blowing from the westward direction. Of course, this could lead to his ships encountering heavy damage, but Nelson was confident that his maneuver would work. The biggest ships led the columns. He led one of them in the *Victory*, while Vice-Admiral Cuthbert Collingwood took charge of the *Royal Sovereign*. The columns fell upon the enemy ships, which were moving rather irregularly in a northern direction. The rear and center of the Franco-Spanish fleet could not withstand the overwhelming onslaught and gave up the battle. The British captured 19 enemy ships, but lost none of theirs. Unfortunately for the British, Vice-Admiral Nelson lost his life while trying to keep Napoleon from concentrating a French fleet in the Channel for invading Great Britain later. Above all, the win at Trafalgar enhanced the global image of Britain as an invincible sea power!

Twice during the course of his engagements with the armies of other countries, Napoleon had felt the need to halt at Vienna, the capital of Austria. Finally, he made it happen in November 1805. His residence in the city was Schonbrunn Palace. The first time that Napoleon entered the palace was on November 14, 1805. Napoleon triumphantly led his soldiers through the winding streets, ensuring that the local populace received a good glimpse of the might of his army. The Emperor of Austria, Francis I, had fled, deserting his people. His palaces and gardens were Napoleon's for the taking. Napoleon was thrilled! Just a couple of months earlier, his army had been encamped on the British Channel, looking for a chance to overcome the English. Now the Viennese elders were tamely handing over the keys of their city to him!

The Battle of Austerlitz was fought between three European emperors. It was the first war of the Third Coalition and turned out to be one of France's greatest victories. When Napoleon and his troops marched into Vienna and occupied it, the Austrian forces moved to another area which today is the modern Czech Republic. Here, they linked up with the Russian forces under the command of General Kutsov. Together, the Austrians and Russians decided to wait for the Prussian army to arrive. For his part, Napoleon did not stay for long in Vienna. He decided to meet his enemies head on, before the Prussians joined them. Despite sweeping aside all manner of opposition, he had to confront several problems. For instance, his men were tired after their long campaign across Europe. They needed rest badly. Napoleon's logistics (management of transport and supplies required for his military operations) were also breaking down. In terms of food, his men were self-reliant enough to confiscate things from the locals whenever they could. Regardless, there was no denying that winter was about to arrive, bringing with it strong winds and snow. The French Army did not have anything like winter quarters where it could settle down.

Therefore, Napoleon needed a rapid battle. He did not want to retreat in the face of bad weather conditions and a shortage of supplies.

The Allies were a combined force of 85,000 soldiers (including cavalry) and 278 guns under the command of Prince Mikhail Kutuzov, a field marshal of the Russian Empire. Along with him, Tsar Alexander of Russia and Emperor Francis I were also present. The Russian commander-in-chief had correctly assessed that Napoleon's army would face difficulties if winter set in and supplies dwindled still further. As a result, he would feel better prepared to face an allied attack during the spring. He was well aware that Napoleon's desire for peaceful negotiations was only a farce. It was his way of luring the Allies into a trap. The Austrian emperor, already in a weak position because of the loss of Vienna and the defeat at Ulm, agreed with Alexander. However, the Russian tsar, who was spoiling for a fight, overrode his field marshal's suggestions and ordered the Allies to confront the approaching French Army without fear. Barring Kutuzov, everyone agreed.

The Allies would wait at the small village of Austerlitz for the French Army to arrive. They also secured some higher ground in the bargain. The majority of the combined forces were Russians. The armies' organization remained similar to the practices of the 18th century. Only aristocrats took charge of the main units or the regiments. They were highly disciplined in their approach and mindset. In case anyone dared to break the rules, he was physically disciplined.

The French Grande Armée was comprised of 73,200 soldiers and 139 guns, all under the command of Napoleon Bonaparte. To the French, numbers did not matter. What mattered was being under the command of highly motivated officers and Napoleon. Additionally, they were highly experienced, intelligent and skilled in battle. After all, the French system awarded commissions purely on merit, without taking lineage or family background into consideration. Over the years, Napoleon had done a lot of reorganizing, as well as initiating reforms with regard to the French officer corps. They were disciplined revolutionaries now!

Both the armies came face to face on the morning of December 2, 1805. The wily Napoleon had positioned a weak group to the right of the main French Army, expecting the Allies to make a rush for this area. He ordered this group to hold on for as long as they could. The Allies were happy to make some headway as they drove the French out from a small hamlet. However, the French right fell back in an orderly manner, all the while inflicting as many casualties as they could on the opposing forces. It helped that the French Army possessed extremely accurate and efficient artillery. As the Austrians and Russians attacked the French right, this artillery not only slowed them down, but also halted their attack completely. Then General Davout arrived with his corps to boost the morale of the French right. At the same time, Napoleon observed that their opponents were so busy tackling the French right that they had forgotten to maintain the strength of their center. Therefore, Napoleon worked out his own strategies. He asked Marshal Lannes' V Corps to take up a position at the northern end of the line, while General Claude Legrand's Corps waited at the southern end. Soult's IV Corps took position in the center.

True, the maneuvers were rather complex in nature, but the French Grand Armée Corps was efficiency personified! They carried out Napoleon's orders speedily and to perfection! Once everyone was in place, Napoleon ordered Davout's corps to attack their opponents' right flank. The Allies never recovered from the sudden assault. Soon enough, the Austrian and Russian troops were in full retreat.

At around 8:45 a.m., Napoleon felt that the center of the Allied troops was sufficiently weak for him to plan another attack. He consulted with Soult about attacking the enemy lines at Pratzen Heights. Just a sudden sharp blow might do the trick. Soult agreed, but his corps could not withstand the brave resistance put up by the Russians. They had to fall back. Then, General Saint-Hillaire stepped in to attack the Russians from higher grounds. As a result, the Allies found their center broken. Both the center and the right of the Allied forces began to flee from the scene. The victorious French pursued them with vigor! Many Russians drowned in a marsh nearby, during their flight. However, Austria's excellent cavalry was able to drive back the less experienced French cavalry, on the left. In fact, they went in for an almost suicidal attack, just to teach the French corps a lesson. As a result, the Allied forces escaped complete annihilation. Around 1,300 French and 15,000 members of the Allied forces lost their lives. Around 6,000 French soldiers suffered severe wounds. The French took thousands of soldiers from the Allied Army as prisoners of war. This battle signaled the end of the wars of the Third Coalition.

Why did the French find it so easy to win at Austerlitz? The primary reason was Napoleon's inherent military genius. He had fooled his enemies into believing that he was weak by offering gestures of peace and peace negotiations. This was evident in the way Tsar Alexander was completely taken in. Then again, the French had employed superior tactics in every battle that they had fought. This was no different! Napoleon could always predict the weak and strong points of his enemies, as well as where and how they would attack. He had passed on this talent to his commanders too. As a result, his army did not even need a complete day to rout the largest of armies! The French Corps had received superior training, such that it could be very flexible. As a result, regardless of whatever sudden changes occurred on battlefield, they could adapt quickly and continue as if nothing had happened.

Unlike the officers of opposing armies, who had acquired their ranks through birth or nobility, the officers in the French Army were battle-hardened veterans who were loyal to the ideals of the French Revolution. Even the French cannons were superior. It helped that wherever and whenever possible, the French did not mind changing their nature of warfare or adhering to outmoded tactics if they would help them win. This time, the Tsar Alexander had brought about the downfall of his troops by not listening to his commander-in-chief. Kutuzov had suggested that if Napoleon and his troops entered deeper into Eastern Europe, it would be possible to weaken him and make the French Army suffer. The final nail in the coffin was the late arrival of the Prussian troops.

Napoleon and Francis II, the Holy Roman Emperor, reached an understanding on December 26, 1805, after France's decisive victories over the Austrians at Ulm and Austerlitz. The countries declared a truce on December 4 and signed the Treaty of Pressburg, also called the Fourth Peace of Pressburg. Charles Maurice de Talleyrand represented France, while Ignaz Gyulai, the Hungarian count, represented Austria. Johann Josef I, the Prince of Liechtenstein, also affixed his signature to the document.

Apart from the clauses focusing on peace and amity, the treaty also demanded Austria's withdrawal from the Third Coalition. Napoleon received substantial territorial gains too, in the form of the reiteration of the Treaties of Campo Formio and Luneville. The Austrians had to hand over their holdings in Bavaria and Italy to France. Napoleon passed on specific Austrian holdings in Germany to his allies. These included the Elector of Baden, the King of Bavaria and the King of Wurttemberg. While Bavaria received Vorarlberg and Tyrol, the Kingdom of Italy received Dalmatia, Venetia and Istria. Bavaria even took control of Augsburg, which had been an independent, free imperial city. In fact, Austria had to give up all claims to everything in the German states.

Napoleon permitted the transfer of the Electorate of Salzburg to Austria as a minor compensation. Emperor Francis II agreed to recognize the royal titles assumed by the Electors of Wurttemberg and

Bavaria. This seemed to signal that the Holy Roman Empire would soon end. Soon after, Napoleon created his Confederation of the Rhine. The Holy Roman Emperor renounced his title of Francis II and instead assumed the title of Emperor Francis I of Austria. France received an indemnity of forty million francs, as per a clause in the treaty.

On July 5, 1806, Napoleon decided to make one of his brothers, Louis, the king of Holland. Louis had previously attended military school at Chalons, France, after the family fled Corsica. He'd been Napoleon's aide-de-camp during the Egyptian campaign and had been governor of Paris since 1805. In return for his royal promotion, Napoleon expected Louis to enforce French navigation laws on all Dutch traders who were engaged in secret deals with Great Britain. Louis, however, refused, stating that such actions would betray Holland's national interests. He exhibited his love for his subjects by initiating wonderful relief efforts during natural, as well as manufactured, disasters. At the same time, he often engaged in erratic and senseless behavior such as changing location of the capital city whenever he felt like it!

On July 12, 1806, Napoleon created a "third" Germany, separate from his two main enemies, Austria and Prussia. Towards this end, he brought about a unification of all his expanded kingdoms, namely, Berg, Bavaria, Hesse-Darmstadt, Wurttemberg, Baden, Nassau and some smaller states. This unified group became the Confederation of the Rhine and was to prove a headache for the whole of Europe until Napoleon's fall from grace in 1813.

Formation of the Fourth Coalition (October 6, 1806)

French influence over the smaller states in Germany was growing. Napoleon brought together the smaller states to create new duchies, electorates and kingdoms. This would aid in smoother governance of non-Prussian Germany. Additionally, Napoleon awarded kingship to the rulers of two of the largest states belonging to the Confederation of the Rhine, Bavaria and Saxony. Such happenings only served to increase the worry of neutral Prussia and other European nations. Napoleon's France was not clear about Prussia's intentions, causing great friction between the former and the latter. A frightened Prussia wanted to have some allies whenever it initiated hostilities against France. Great Britain was supportive of Prussia's aims and Russia was eager to avenge its most recent losses. Therefore, Prussia, Russia and Great Britain came together to form the Fourth Coalition on October 6, 1806, which lasted through July 1807.

The Battles

Jena was a city in Germany, lying in the valley of the Saale River. This battle took place between the French Grandee Armée and the Prussian Army on a plateau that lay northwest of Jena. After signing a secret pact with Russia in July 1806, Frederick

William III of Prussia decided to initiate war with Napoleon. Towards this end, he dispatched 35,000 soldiers under the command of Prince Hohenlohe towards the eastern part of this plateau. These men were part of the Prussian Flank Guard, which was ensuring that the retreat of the main Army in the northeast, under the command of the seventy-year-old Duke of Brunswick (Charles William Ferdinand), took place without any mishaps along the way. Queen Louise of Prussia had made a personal request that the duke return to take charge of the forces, despite his age.

Now, Hohenlohe believed that his men just had to deal with a French flank guard. Napoleon, on the other hand, believed that his 90,000 men had to reach a small and unoccupied plateau by crossing the Saale River through Jena and climbing wooded and steep slopes, prior to launching an attack on the main Prussian Army. Therefore, after reaching the place on the night of October 13, Napoleon ordered the French Corps, under the leadership of General Lannes, to climb up onto the plateau. They were to attack the Prussian Army at 6:30 a.m. on October 14, 1806. Napoleon did not want the enemy to take the initiative, drive Lannes' men off the plateau and trap them against the Saale River. However, the Prussian prince did not take the French presence seriously and failed to offer a full-out defense. As a result, the French overwhelmed the Prussians from all sides.

General Augereau's corps attacked from the left, Soult's men from Lannes' right and Ney's forces remained between Augereau and Lannes. In the midst of the battle, it seemed that the Prussians were getting back on their feet, thanks to General Ney, who initiated a premature and unplanned surprised counterattack serious enough to disturb the French troops in the center. However, when Napoleon arrived at 1:00 p.m. to join the four French Corps, along with General Murat's cavalry and the Imperial Guard, the Prussians in the center and on the right had to take to their heels! General Ruchel of Prussia arrived at that moment with another 15,000 men but their counterattack proved to be of little help. Even the valiant Prussian left suffered, due to the defeat of the main army. As a result, the Prussians lost over 25,000 soldiers, while France lost around 5,000.

The Prussians and the French fought another battle simultaneously, along with the Battle of Jena, on October 14, 1806—the Battle of Auerstadt. The main Prussian Army, comprised of 60,000 men, engaged in a war with Marshall Davout's III Corps of the French Grande Armée, comprising 27,000 soldiers. The Prussian leaders were the Duke of Brunswick and King Frederick William III. According to the

French plans, Davout, along with Bernadotte, was to prevent the main Prussian Army from engaging in battle with Napoleon's army.

Davout urged his small force to move rapidly towards the strategic Pass of Kosen near Auerstadt village, which lay in the northeast. Davout launched his attack at 6:00 a.m., wherein the French fought in a coordinated and disciplined fashion. The Prussians, in contrast, offered ill-coordinated and piecemeal replies. For one thing, they did not come together to apply their joint strength against the French Army. Secondly, their artillery, cavalry and infantry failed to work in harmony. Then again, Davout's army was quick-thinking. When the Prussian Blucher's cavalry pushed the opponents into squares, the latter had no artillery or infantry to support them. Yet these soldiers had received such superb drilling that they refused to be cowed. They simply modified their formations within the squares, in order to counter the Prussians in the most efficient ways possible.

The Prussians received another blow midmorning, when their experienced leader, the Duke of Brunswick, died. King Frederick William III did not prove to be an effective substitute, as a commander. Thus, by 12:30, Davout's army managed to flank the Prussian Army on both sides, as well as push them towards the place where the remnants of Prince

Hohenlohe's army were fighting. His intelligent leadership, combined with the superior operational and tactical skills of his soldiers, caused the destruction of the Prussian Army. True, the losses were rather heavy on both sides, with the French losing around 11,000 men and the Prussians losing around 13,000. However, the Prussians lost 175 guns too. Thus, France succeeded in knocking the Prussians out of the war.

Soon after defeating the Prussians, Napoleon made a grand entry into Berlin, the capital of Prussia. It was a great triumph for the French, since they had defeated an equally powerful enemy. In those days, the world categorized Russia, Great Britain, the Habsburg Empire, Prussia and France as Europe's greatest powers.

Napoleon's entry was something of a spectacle for the Prussian public though Napoleon's uniform was humble, akin to that of a colonel's. Of course, he had his unadorned bicorn hat on his head. Unlike him, his marshals—Augereau, Berthier and Davout—wore gold-embroidered uniforms and hats. As the four rode into Berlin, an honor guard comprised of cuirassiers escorted them. Cuirassiers refer to cavalrymen wearing breastplates (cuirasses). As the group entered the city, the highest functionaries came forward with the keys of the city in their hands. This indicated their submission to a superior authority.

Napoleon wanted more, especially after tasting success. He felt that if he closed the continent to British ships and products, he would destroy the country's commercial gains. If the British found it difficult to dispose of their manufactured goods, the economy of the nation would suffer. There would be rampant unemployment and overproduction of goods. Britain's treasury would become devoid of the foreign gold wending its way to it via the country's flourishing export trade. This would allow France to penetrate Britain's foreign markets. In turn, the severe economic crisis would force Great Britain to seek peace with France.

Great Britain offered money to European monarchies for fielding armies against France. This funding helped Britain keep up a flourishing export and re-export trade, for they had many routes at their disposal to transport goods. In order to stop this trade, Napoleon issued the Berlin Decrees on November 21, 1806. According to these decrees, Great Britain was supposed to be blockaded. Therefore, no ships coming from Great Britain or any of her colonies were supposed to enter a port directly under the control of France. Trading could not take place even if the products/goods arrived via neutral ships.

In retaliation, Britain demanded that all neutral ships halt at its ports for inspection, as well as for acquiring trading licenses. Napoleon declared that he would seize any seagoing vessel that dared to halt at an English port. Thus, the neutrals found themselves entangled in a naval war not of their own making! Additionally, this kind of economic warfare affected trade across Europe. Even the French suffered, along with their allies, since they had depended heavily on the British colonies for obtaining raw materials. With the collapse of ancillary industries, such as sugar refining and shipbuilding, the famous Atlantic ports of Amsterdam, Nantes and Bordeaux suffered tremendous losses. European trade made a decision to shift inland, since there was no other option.

What did this Continental System do to Great Britain's economy? Well, it did strain it a good deal, bringing down the gold reserves, as well as reducing exports. However, the British had an advantage in that Europeans were generally fond of British goods. Therefore, smugglers still managed to transport their goods from one place to another, albeit through places like Portugal and Spain. Napoleon became busy in distributing his troops to places, where there seemed to be evasions against the blockade. This distribution caused the numbers in the main army to dwindle.

Napoleon's Grand Armée had been residing in its winter quarters in Poland for almost a month. Suddenly, in late January 1807, the Russians, under the leadership of Levin August Count von Bennigsen, initiated an offensive against the left wing of the French. They shifted a major part of their army north, towards East Prussia. The Russian army commander also placed a Prussian Corps on his right. While positioning his troops, Count von Bennigsen encountered Marshal Michel Ney and his VI Corps. Ney had gone against Napoleon's orders and gone north, far beyond the assigned winter cantonments. It was easy to defeat Ney and his troops.

Next, the Russians encountered the isolated French Corps commanded by Marshal Jean-Baptiste Bernadotte. Bernadotte's men engaged in tough fighting, managed to escape serious injuries and retreated to the southwest. When Napoleon heard about these goings on, he decided to turn the situation to France's advantage. He sent word to Bernadotte to move away from Bennigsen's army, while the balance of the French Grande Armée moved northwards. This way, Napoleon hoped to attack the left flank of the Russians and prevent their retreat to the east. However, the messenger, who was carrying the emperor's plans to Bernadotte, fell into the hands of a band of Cossacks. They were quick to pass on Napoleon's plans to Bennigsen. While Bernadotte remained unaware of what was happening, the Russian troops beat a hasty retreat to the village of Jonkowo!

While Bennigsen was hurriedly reassembling his men at Jonkowo on February 3, Marshal Nicolas Soult's IV Corps came up on his left and rear. There was a clash, which led to some casualties. Soult took over the county of Allenstein/Olsztyn and thereafter guided his men in a northern direction along the eastern bank of the River Alle. Bennigsen faced trouble from the south, too, where Marshal Pierre Augereau and his VII Corps, as well as Ney's troops, stood at the ready. The Russian Kamensky lay in wait on the western bank of the River, along with four Russian battalions and three Prussian artillery batteries. Regardless, the French managed to capture the village of Bergfried and the bridge. The Russians managed to recapture the bridge for some time, but lost it again. Bennigsen beat a retreat to the north first, and then towards the northeast. However, wherever his troops went, the French remained in hot pursuit. Finally, Bennigsen moved to the town of Preussisch-Eylau, resolving to make a stand there. He could afford to be confident of victory, for his forces were concentrated in one place. Napoleon, on the other hand, had allowed his army to spread out more widely than was his usual wont, due to the savagery of the winter weather and the terrible state of the roads in Poland.

The Russian Army was comprised of 67,000 soldiers and possessed 460 guns. In contrast, Napoleon's French Grande Armée had 45,000 men and 200 guns. Napoleon planned to take his men to higher lands, to the west of Eylau. He would not initiate any attack, but instead, waited for the Russians to do so. At the same time, he asked Ney's troops to support him on the northern flank, while Davout's troops took care of the southern one. However, before anything could happen, the French train, including Napoleon's personal staff too, got lost. As a result, the move towards Eylau ended in an action-packed night on the evening of February 7, 1807.

Napoleon's army and the forces staffing the Russian outposts engaged in a bitter battle. As more and more troops joined in from both sides, the battle escalated out of control. Finally, the corps under the control of Augereau, Murat and Soult took over the town. They managed to find better shelter than the other troops. However, the losses were equally heavy on both sides, approximately 4,000 each.

February 8, 1807, brought with it several snowstorms. The Battle of Eylau began in earnest with an aggressive artillery duel. Soult's Corps up with an attack on the center of the Russian army. The idea was to keep the Russians in one place, until Davout and Ney arrived with their respective

Corps. Napoleon only had 41,000 men with him, while the Russian troops now numbered 63,000. Bennigsen's men launched a counterattack. Napoleon sent Augereau towards the south center, in the hope that his troops would give adequate support to Soult, who was under immense pressure. However, Augereau's men lost their way in the snowstorm. They stumbled onto a duel going on between the grand batteries of the Russians and their own French Army. The Russian guns were engaging in heavy fire, prompting the French to respond. However, the French were firing blindly. Naturally, few survived.

Napoleon had no one left, barring Murat's cavalry. He had to restore the French center, as well as save the survivors belonging to Augereau's Corps. Murat lived up to Napoleon's faith! His cavalry barged through the Russian center, forcing it to split into two columns. Then his cavalry raced towards the Russian rear in a single column, turned and plunged through the center once again. These moves ensured that the Russians were unable to re-form their lines ever again. As a result, Napoleon was able to hold on to his center for at least six hours, until reinforcements arrived for both sides. The combined forces of Davout and Ney totaled 26,000 men. General Lestroq brought along 9,000 Prussians as reinforcements. Murat also captured around seventy guns. However, in the process, he had to sacrifice 1,500 men from his army of 10,000.

When Davout arrived, he placed his troops on the southern Russian left flank. Napoleon wanted the attack to commence at 1:00 p.m. By 3:30 p.m., the Russians found themselves at the losing end as their lines reached breaking point. Fortunately for them, the timely arrival of reinforcements saved them. Davout found himself outflanked by the arrival of the Prussians. Ney arrived at 8:00 p.m. and attacked the Russians' left flank in the north. The forces went on battling even after dark. The parties stopped only when they were too exhausted to continue. Soon after the battle ended at 10:00 p.m., Bennigsen withdrew his forces from the battlefield. The French Army was too tired to pursue them. Neither side could claim a victory, considering that the losses were dreadfully heavy. While the French lost about 10,000 men on February 8, the Russians and Prussians lost 25,000. No one could keep track of the wounded, as the injured soldiers simply froze to death in the snow. The Battle of Eylau went down in history as one of the most horrific and bloodiest Napoleonic Wars.

Siege of Danzig (March 18 – 27 May, 1807)

The Prussians had suffered badly at the hands of the French Army during both the Battle of Jena and the Battle of Auerstadt. In fact, they barely had any main armies left. Regardless, the Prussians refused to give in to the French. Even after retreating to their residence in East Prussia, they looked towards their Russian allies to help them out of the crisis. It helped that the Prussians were still in control of several fortresses, including the highly important Baltic Port of Danzig.

Napoleon had tried to organize a winter campaign against the Russians. However, the campaign had turned into an expensive and viciously bloody affair, as witnessed at Eylau. This was the first time that the French Emperor had experienced a military setback on land. It placed him in a dangerously isolated position in the midst of Eastern Europe. At least Austria was quiet, after suffering a crushing defeat at the Battle of Austerlitz. As for the Germans, some remained opposed to him, and some remained his allies. However, if the French experienced anymore defeats, even their allies would begin to oppose them. Therefore, with nothing much to do, Napoleon spent the winter creating a new army in Germany. He also hired new recruits to join the French Army, in order to replace those who had died.

Napoleon formed a novel multi-national X Corps. He placed a highly experienced, respected veteran of several wars, Republican Marshal Lefebvre, in charge. This corps was comprised of two divisions each from Poland, Italy and France (Menard). There were also troops from Posen and Saxony. There was no time to test this unit to see if it was fit for front-line service or not. Yet the supremely confident Napoleon felt that the X Corps would handle the Siege of Danzig well. Furthermore, the French emperor wanted to know if Lefebvre would justify his place in the Imperial Peerage or not. Suffice to say that Lefebvre conducted himself impeccably throughout the siege!

Danzig was nestled on the southern bank of the River Vistula, close to the Baltic Coast. The River Vistula moved west in alignment with the coastline, prior to turning north at Danzig. Then, the river split, in order to meander around the Island of Helm, before mingling with the sea at Neufahrwasser. Although the British Royal Navy had a squadron in the Baltic region, it was nowhere near Danzig, which was three miles inland. Therefore, it was not necessary to take command of the sea, in order to initiate a Siege of Danzig. Regardless, Napoleon divided his French Army into two, near the River Vistula. As for Lefebvre himself, he had around 20,000 men under his command. The reserve forces were ready to provide necessary support to him, whenever required. They were under the twin command of Lannes and Mortier.

Danzig's protector, and France's opposition, was General Kalkreuth. He was in charge of 14,400 infantry, 1,600 cavalry, twenty-six mortars, 303 guns and twenty howitzers. Additionally, his troops would never run short of supplies, since Danzig was a major port in the area.

Lefebvre began his preparations for the Siege of Danzig on February 18, 1807. When they were ready, his troops moved towards the port in early March. They encountered Prussian outposts along the way. By March 11, they had tackled every single one of them. The French formally invaded Danzig on March 18, 1807. Then Lefebvre focused his main efforts on the western part of Danzig. The French finished the first parallel by April 2 and initiated work on the second parallel on April 11. The French also set up a second combination of works on the southwestern side of Danzig. Although the brave Prussians went in for a sortie on April 11, it did not help. The French refused to slow down their work.

By April 14, even the second parallel was complete. After this, the French set up various fortifications on the north of the River Vistula between April 15 and April 17. These fortifications faced the Prussian positions at the mouth of River Vistula. By April 24, the heavy batteries were in position to begin firing. The Prussians carried out another sortie on April 26. Yet the French managed to complete the third parallel by April 29. Everything went according to plan and on May 7, the French Army took over Helm Island. This way, they stood guard over the river route that lay between Danzig and the coast.

The Russians arrived on May 10, under the command of General Kamenskoi. They numbered 8,000. The troops landed at Neufahrwasser on the coast. They had no choice, for the French had blocked the river route. While Kamenskoi rested for four days, Lannes went ahead with his preparations. He took the nearest troops to the front, positioning them in place by May 12. When the Russians finally launched their attack on May 14, they found the route blocked by French forces under the twin command of General Schramm and General Gardenne. Kamenskoi's army moved along the narrow spit of land that lay between River Vistula and the open sea, hoping to wrest Helm Island from the French. However, the leading troops, whom Lannes had positioned in front, managed to hold off the Russians long enough for reinforcements to arrive, along with Lannes and Oudinot. This was enough to beat back the Russians. They had to retreat, after losing 1,500 men.

All this while, the garrison of Danzig remained inactive. They did carry out another sortie on May 20, but the move came too late to stop Danzig from falling into French hands. On May 21, Marshal

Mortier and his corps fought alongside Lefebvre, thereby bringing the total number of soldiers to 47,900. On May 22, Lefebvre sent across an envoy to dictate terms of surrender to General Kalkreuth. Both sides initiated talks. Napoleon made it clear that he would resume the offensive on June 10 if the talks did not yield fruitful results. In fact, he was willing to offer generous terms if Danzig surrendered before that. Kalkreuth capitulated. On May 27, 1807, Danzig's garrison marched out with the full honors of war. The French escorted them to the Prussian outposts at Pillau. Danzig's garrison had agreed not to launch any attacks against the French or the allies of France for a full year. A relieved Napoleon would now be able to focus on the Russians.

Since his winter campaigns had not yielded highly fruitful results, Napoleon decided to take full advantage of spring. He was keen to renew his campaign against the Russians. After the fall of Danzig, he was still planning his strategies when Levin August Count von Bennigsen and his troops began to converge on Marshal Michel Ney's exposed VI Corps on June 2. The battle continued for two days as Ney and his 17,000 men strove to carry on a rearguard action against 63,000 Russians. The French Corps lost its baggage train and two guns and suffered 2,042 casualties. Yet Ney and the majority of his soldiers managed to escape via the

Pasleka River, towards the southwest. Bennigsen could only curse himself for a missed opportunity!

Two days later, Napoleon ordered his 190,000-strong army to converge upon 100,000 Russians and 15,000 Prussians. Bennigsen had sensed the approach of the avalanche and therefore directed his men to retreat to Heilsberg, located on the River Lyna/Alle. He then ordered his men to take up defensive positions across town. When the French Army arrived on June 10, under the command of Marshals Lannes and Murat, Bennigsen's men were able to repulse several attacks. The French casualties were huge. Despite having the capacity to hold the lines, the Russians decided to move towards Friedland on the following day. The Russians had to cross the River Alle and enter the town, which lay on its west bank. Friedland was a small region between a mill strip and the river. General Dmitry Golitsyn, the head of the Russian cavalry, cleared the region around Friedland of French outposts on June 13. The French had been pursuing them, and this led to the decisive Battle of Friedland.

Napoleon had divided his main army into several columns, enabling it to travel diverse routes. Marshal Jean Lannes was the first to arrive in Friedland. He confronted Russian troops to the west of the town, just a few hours after midnight, on

June 14, 1807. The battle began in earnest in front of the village of Posthenen and Sortlack Wood. As the battle progressed vigorously, each side tried to extend its line northwards, towards Heinrichsdorf. The French won the race when Marquis de Grouchy and his cavalry occupied the village.

Meanwhile, Bennigsen kept adding to his forces by pushing men across the river. By 6:00 a.m., he had a huge army of 50,000 on standby. When one section of his troops was battling Lannes, he deployed other soldiers along the southern part of the Heinrichsdorf-Friedland Road. The line stretched towards the upper bends of the River Alle. Some more troops moved north, towards Schwonau. A reserve cavalry took up position to support the men engaged in battle with the French in Sortlack Wood. As time passed, Lannes began to find it very difficult to hold on to his position. However, Marshal Edouard Mortier and his VIII Corps arrived on time at Heinrichsdorf. The corps forced the Russians to leave Schwonau. The French forces received further support from the arrival of Napoleon with reinforcements. He positioned Marshal Michel Ney and his VI Corps to take up a stand, south of Lannes, between Sortlack Wood and Posthenen. Marshal Claude Victor-Perrin and his corps, along with the Imperial Guard, stood to the west of Posthenen. They were the reserve forces. Grouchy and Mortier, with their respective groups, took up positions as the French left. Thus, by 5:00 p.m., Napoleon managed to form his troops. All the while, the French artillery ensured that no one came to any harm. After assessing the confined terrain around Friedland, Napoleon decided to attack the Russian left.

With a huge artillery barrage in front of them, Marshal Ney and his men moved towards Sortlack Wood. It did not take them long to drive the Russians back. Similarly, General Jean Gabriel Marchand and his men attacked the Russians on the far left. They drove them into the River Alle near Sortlack Wood. The Russian cavalry then stepped in, determined to rout Marchand's left. However, Marquis de Latour-Maubourg and his dragoons surged forward to meet the cavalry and managed to repulse them. Ney and his men continued to push the Russians towards the upper bend of the Alle. By this time, the sun was setting. However, Napoleon wanted a decisive victory. He would not let the Russians escape. Therefore, he ordered General Pierre Dupont to take a division of the reserve forces and attack the Russian Army. Dupont received help from the French Cavalry too, which repulsed the Russian Cavalry.

Due to Napoleon's actions, the battle began in earnest once again. General Alexandre-Antoine de Senarmont used his artillery at close range so skillfully that he simply tore into the enemy lines. Soon enough, the Russians were fleeing through the streets of Friedland. As for the southern side of the field, Ney's men pursued the fleeing Russians, turning it into a complete rout. Once they had finished successfully attacking the Russian left, Mortier and Lannes advanced, focused on pinning the Russian right and Russian center. In his turn, Dupont shifted his attack to the north and forded the millstream. Then, he launched an attack on the flank of the Russian center. Despite fighting fiercely, the Russians had to give in at the end and retreat. The Russian right managed to escape by taking the Allenburg Road. The remainder of the Russian Army, however, had to cross the River Alle in order to escape. Many soldiers drowned in the process.

The Russians suffered approximately 300,000 casualties, while the French incurred just about 100,000. The outcome of this terrible warfare was that after the Russians had lost about a third of their army, Tsar Alexander decided to discuss peace. When the French were heading towards River Nieman, the tsar sent his envoys to Napoleon's camp. The envoys offered an armistice from June 23 onwards. It would continue for four weeks. The Russian Tsar and the French Emperor came face to face for the first time on June 25. The meeting took place on a raft in the middle of the River Niemen!

Treaties of Tilsit (July 7 and July 9, 1807)

With the Treaties of Tilsit on July 7 and 9, 1807, the wars of the Fourth Coalition ended. The negotiations continued for two weeks, finally resulting in two treaties. One was with Russia, and the other was with Prussia. The treaty with Russia was comprised of secret terms that brought about an alliance between France and Russia. In contrast, the treaty with Prussia was public, as well as humiliating in nature.

Russia affixed its signature on the Treaty of Tilsit on July 7, 1807. As per the treaty's public terms/articles, Russia agreed to grant the city of Danzig freedom. However, it would still receive protection from the King of Prussia and the King of Saxony. Of course, France would be the real power behind the thrones. Napoleon also offered the King of Saxony another gift—he would force Prussia to give up all her Polish provinces. These territories became ten new states, which comprised the Grand Duchy of Warsaw, on July 19, 1807. The King of Saxony, Frederick August, would rule this dukedom. The Poles were pleased, for Prince Frederick had ascended the throne of Poland via a legal constitution on May 3, 1791. At that time, the Poles had abolished the election of kings. Even the free city of Danzig became part of this duchy.

More territories would become part of the Grand Duchy of Warsaw in 1809, when Napoleon forced Austria to give up its gains from the third partition of Poland. Thus, the duchy doubled in size to 2,400,000 inhabitants. The grateful Poles hoped to live in a reunited Poland later, thanks to Napoleon's efforts. However, they were not to know, that even in this case, Napoleon was using them for his personal gains. By having more and more nations depend upon his benevolence, he hoped to increase his sphere of influence in Europe to such an extent, that nothing could come in the way of his acquiring a world empire and him becoming a world emperor!

After forming the Grand Duchy of Warsaw, Napoleon enforced his Napoleonic Code in the dukedom. He also introduced mandatory military service via the code. The duchy created a new constitution, wherein serfdom faced abolishment. The constitution extended the franchise too. With the separation of the church from the state, the former acquired the label of a private institution. The Napoleonic Code introduced a civil registry too.

However, frequent wars were to prove a humongous economic burden. Furthermore, the duchy had to hire new recruits, in order to replace the soldiers who had lost their lives in battle. In this area, the duchy could not complain much, for the Poles were obliged to remain loyal to Napoleon until the end.

Furthermore, Napoleon himself looked after everything with regard to the Grand Duchy of Warsaw's army. He wanted to ensure that 800 Poles would equal the power of 8,000 enemy soldiers! Some of the Polish citizens were so loyal to Napoleon that they even followed him into exile to Elba, a few years later!

Following the establishment of Warsaw's Grand Duchy, Napoleon was ready to appoint Russia as France's mediator with Great Britain. However, there was a condition attached to this agreement. Tsar Alexander would have to publicly recognize Joseph Bonaparte as the King of Naples and Louis Bonaparte as the King of Holland. Russia would also have to award equal respect to Jerome Bonaparte, Napoleon's youngest brother, as the King of Westphalia, a kingdom Napoleon planned to create for him. This would be comprised of a mix of former Russian provinces that lay to the west of the River Elbe, as well as other French-controlled German states. The pleasure-loving Jerome would remain in charge of this kingdom until 1813. Apart from this, Napoleon and Russia agreed to official recognition of the Confederation of the Rhine and the titles of all the members belonging to this confederation. Finally, the Russians agreed to let France act as a mediator in their war against the Ottoman Turks. Once formal peace came into effect, the Russians would retreat from Moldavia and Wallachia.

Both the emperors had some secret terms/articles included in the treaty too. According to these agreements, there would be an alliance between Russia and France, wherein they would help each other in war. If other European powers threatened either one's well-being, the other would lend adequate strength and support. If the British government refused to agree to Russian mediation, Russia would withdraw its ambassador from Great Britain. Similarly, Tsar Alexander would use his influential powers in convincing Sweden, Denmark and Portugal to prevent British ships from entering their respective ports. In case these nations refused the mediation, Russia, along with France, would declare war upon them. In return for this support, France would provide Russia all the necessary help for confronting the Ottomans. The French Army would also help Russia in seizing all of the Ottoman Empire's European provinces, barring Roumalia and Constantinople.

Napoleon was not so kind to Prussia when the second treaty was signed on July 9, 1807. Napoleon seized the opportunity to take away all Poland's lands, as well as everything to the west of the River Elbe. Prussia had to remain content with its original borders of 1772. Napoleon took away the Fortress of

Magdeburg too. The ruler of Prussia, Frederick William III, had to agree to recognize the rulers and the kingdoms of Naples, Holland and Westphalia. He had to award equal importance to the Confederation of the Rhine too. Whatever treaties had existed before between Prussia and the states lying to the west of the River Elbe became invalid. The only secret article/term mentioned in this treaty was Prussia's agreement to join Napoleon's army whenever it went to war against Great Britain. Prussia would suffer further humiliation on July 12, 1807, via the signing of another treaty. According to this treaty, Prussia would have to accept the presence of the French Army on its lands, until it had paid a war indemnity. Napoleon set this war indemnity at 140 million francs.

Napoleon could gloat over what he had achieved via the Treaties of Tilsit! They placed him at the peak of his powers, wherein he dominated major parts of Europe. His domain spread from France to the Russian border. It penetrated Italy too. However, he was not to know that the Prussians would not take everything lying down. In fact, they would just bide their time until the right moment to strike. Even France's "friendship" with Russia would experience strain in a couple of years or so when it failed to provide sufficient support to Napoleon during France's war with Austria in 1809. Furthermore, the Continental System continued to affect Russia's trade. Thus, regardless of the Treaties of Tilsit, France and Russia would be at war after a few years, thereby ending Napoleon's career in a disastrous manner.

Treaty of Fontainebleau (October 27, 1807)

Even after France's victorious Treaties of Tilsit, the world still acknowledged Great Britain's mastery over the seas. However, British leaders began to suspect that Napoleon might use his gift of oratory to convince Russian, Danish and Swedish fleets to join him in his battle against the British. Furthermore, the British leaders wanted to protect their valuable trading interests in the Baltic region, for this was an extremely vital source for naval supplies. With these considerations in mind, Great Britain decided to launch a large expedition of its own. Gathering 29,000 troops and over 400 transports and warships, the Royal Navy launched a secret mission. Without giving a hint of where they were heading, the British ships set sail. By August 1807, the naval forces had reached the shores of Denmark. At first, the British just demanded that the Danes give up their fleet to the British without resisting. The Danes refused, thereby initiating hostilities. Thus, Great Britain attacked Copenhagen.

When the British troops landed near Copenhagen, their commander Arthur Wellesley (who would later become the First Duke of Wellington) positioned them in strategic places. This way, they surrounded the entire city. He initiated negotiations, but they did not progress due to the stubborn resistance offered by the Danes. Therefore, on September 2, 1807, Admiral James Gambier ordered the British fleet to begin bombarding the city. They used Congreve rockets freely. This was the first time that rockets had come into play in European warfare. Soon enough, Copenhagen was in flames and there were heavy civilian casualties. The Danes had little left in the way of choices. They surrendered their fleet to the British on September 7, 1807.

When the British left, they took sixty Danish ships, as well as large quantities of naval supplies. While the British suffered just 200 casualties (wounded/dead), the Danes suffered 2,000 to 3,000 casualties (all dead). Over the next six years or so, Denmark and Great Britain would remain at war with each other. The Danes managed to capture a few British merchant ships, forcing the British to send escort ships along with their merchant conveys during Baltic trading. However, the countries never engaged in land battles ever again. Only minor clashes at sea continued.

As per his Berlin Decrees, issued back in November 1806, Napoleon had, for years, been urging all European nations to join in a continental blockade which would prevent trading of British goods throughout Europe. Not all countries were in agreement with his ideas, especially Portugal, which had always been a longtime ally of Great Britain. Therefore, Napoleon decided that he needed to teach this country a lesson. But if he was to invade Portugal, he needed to move his ground troops through Spain. This would become possible only if he signed a treaty with Spain. However, Jean-Andoche Junot's army had already entered Spain before the signing of the Treaty of Fontainebleau on October 27, 1807.

This treaty was a secret agreement between King Charles IV of Spain and Napoleon. According to the treaty, the combined forces of Spain and France would strive to drive the House of Braganza from the Kingdom of Portugal. After this, they would divide the country into three regions. The plenipotentiary of King Charles IV was Don Eugenio Izquierdo. The representative of Emperor Napoleon Bonaparte was Marshal Geraud Duroc. The plenipotentiary and representative engaged in negotiations, prior to preparing a document containing fourteen articles. There were supplementary provisions too, related to the allocation of troops for the proposed invasion of Portugal. However, anyone knowing Napoleon well would suggest that it was altogether possible that he did not intend to carry out all of the conditions mentioned in the treaty! After all, it would have been to his advantage to place large numbers of French troops in Spain, such that he could take over the country some day.

As per the treaty, once France and Spain defeated Portugal, they would split it into three sections—the Entre-Douro-e-Minho Province, the Principality of the Algarves and a cluster of remaining provinces and overseas territories under Portugal's control. The king of Etruria would take charge of the province, in exchange for handing over Tuscany to the French. The Portuguese territories lay in between the Douro River and Minho River. In other words, the King of Etruria would have control over the Kingdom of Northern Lusitania. D. Manuel Godoy, the Spanish minister, would control the Principality of the Algarves, which encompassed the Province of Alentejo and the former Kingdom of Algarve. As for the rest of the provinces and overseas territories, France and Spain would see to their division later.

The House of Braganza ruled Portugal in 1807 and Prince John held all the powers in his hands. He was the Prince Regent, since his mother, Queen Marie I, was believed to be insane. The Prince Regent aimed to preserve Portuguese neutrality, regardless of whatever happened in the rest of Europe. Napoleon and King Charles IV of Spain approached him on August 12, 1807. They demanded that Portugal declare war on Great Britain. They also wanted the Portuguese fleet to link up with the Franco-Spanish fleets, the arrest of all British subjects who resided in Portugal and suggested that the Prince Regent seize all British goods flooding the country. It should have gladdened Napoleon's heart when Prince John appeared willing to break off all diplomatic relations, as well as trading ties, with Great Britain. However, Napoleon had not come there for the sole purpose of enforcing the Continental System on Portugal. He had other plans, which the Prince Regent was unaware of at that time.

Napoleon was amassing a large number of French troops on the borders of Spain. The first group was comprised of the Corps of Observation of the Gironde. General Andoche Junot was in charge of the 25,000-strong Army. Junot's army entered Spain via its border on October 18, heading towards Salamanca. En route, French engineers took note of every post that could be of military significance. Meanwhile, Napoleon placed a second Corps of Observation of the Gironde at Bayonne. This corps would cross over into Spain, too, sometime later. Napoleon was quite leisurely in his actions! However, a crisis erupted at the Spanish Court which made him realize that he had better hurry up with his plans. King Charles IV had his son arrested on October 27, accusing him of treason. Within the same week, the king pardoned his son. Thereafter, the affairs that took place during this frantic week acquired the label of the Affair of the Escurial. A disturbed Napoleon decided that it was time to depose the Bourbon Dynasty that controlled Spain.

When Junot's army reached Salamanca on November 12, Napoleon sent orders for him to pick up his pace. The emperor also ordered him to alter the route of the invasion, so he would no longer take the road that went past the Almeida Fortress. Instead, Junot would move south, crossing the Estremadura Mountains, prior to entering Portugal along the line of the Tagus River. This new route was quite barren and sparsely populated. Furthermore, Junot's army had to traverse a number of rough, mountainous routes. The trek was tough. Therefore, when the French Army finally reached Alcantara on the Tagus River, just five days after leaving Ciudad Rodrigo, it was not really equipped to deal with a strong enemy. The army had lost half of its horses along the way and only had six remaining guns in its possession. A desperate General Junot seized supplies and ammunitions from a Spanish army encampment stationed at Alcantara, prior to heading west and towards Portugal.

The first of Junot's troops stepped into Abrantes on November 23, a good eleven days after leaving Salamanca. The last of his troops filed in on November 26. Fortunately for the bedraggled French troops, the Portuguese barely put up any kind of resistance. Otherwise, Junot's troops would have found themselves in serious trouble. No reinforcements could reach them on time, for it was necessary to travel for four days along mountainous routes, prior to reaching Abrantes. It helped that no Portuguese troops were in sight anywhere! Instead, only a Portuguese diplomat, Barreto, was around. He offered tribute and offers of submission to the French Army. An emboldened Junot then decided to make a calculated gamble. He selected the least disorganized companies from his army and organized them into four impromptu brigades comprising 1,500 men. Junot decided to use them to invade Lisbon. Junot's occupation of Lisbon became the first campaign in what the world would come to refer to as the Peninsular War.

Junot's brigades entered Lisbon on November 30, 1807. Once again, he had an easy takeover, as the Portuguese populace offered little resistance. Over the next few days, the remaining stragglers of his army, whom he had left behind at Abrantes, joined him. However, it would take quite some time to regroup his cavalry or artillery. Nonetheless, the French settled down in Lisbon quite comfortably.

The surprising lack of resistance from the Portuguese was because Prince John and his advisors had never believed that Napoleon would plan an invasion against their country. By the time they woke up to his plans, it was too late to offer any form of fight. The confusion only increased when a British fleet appeared off Lisbon, prior to Junot's arrival. Over the next few days, the Prince Regent remained in a state of confusion. Should he submit to the French? Should he flee the country? The British fleet was under the command of Sir Sydney Smith, who had just one main concern. He wished to capture the Portuguese fleet of fifteen ships. Therefore, he strove to convince Prince John to flee to Brazil, in order to remain safe from French capture. At this time, the prince also received a copy of the *Moniteur*, a publication from Paris. In it, Napoleon made a public announcement of his plans to depose the House of Braganza. This sufficed to convince the Prince Regent that he was better off elsewhere. On November 29, Prince John and his mother fled the country. Thousands of Portuguese citizens did the same.

Junot's army was not alone in its invasion of Lisbon. Napoleon had sent along two Spanish armies too. However, their movements had been slow, even slower than Junot's army. They entered Lisbon only after it had already fallen into French hands. The southern army reached Lisbon on December 2 and

Oporto on December 13. Although the Portuguese in Lisbon had not offered much opposition in the beginning, they did revolt on December 13. Junot's men took care of the rioters quite efficiently. After this, Junot disbanded the Portuguese army. He sent around 6,000 to 7,000 inexperienced soldiers, in the form of a single force, to the Baltic. The sudden French invasion left a bad taste in Portugal's mouth, but for the moment, the Portuguese were helpless. They lacked leadership and direction to counter the French Army. It was only when the Spaniards revolted against the French presence on their soil, during the spring of 1808, that the Portuguese initiated a true insurrection. Soon after, the British intervened and helped the Portuguese drive the French from Portugal.

There was no denying that the commanders of the French Army were highly skilled in battle and had gained vast experience over the years. However, they had failed to understand that the Spaniards' views of social, political and religious lives could be very inflammatory indeed! Things would have been fine if Napoleon had left well enough alone following the Treaties of Tilsit and his invasions of Portugal and Spain. However, Napoleon could never stop himself from meddling in other people's affairs. This time he interfered unwisely with Spanish royal politics. In fact, he interfered to such an extent that the Spanish monarch had to vacate his throne! Napoleon expressed the opinion that his older brother, Joseph Bonaparte, would be a better choice for the position of Emperor of Spain. To that end, he incarcerated Ferdinand VII and Charles IV. The latter was the father of the former, the current ruler of Spain. Napoleon forced these Bourbon rulers to renounce all claims to their own throne.

Such actions did not go down well with the people of Spain. Things came to a head when Marshal Joachim Murat began to prepare for sending all the children belonging to the Royal Family of Spain to France. Even though the French had been in control of Madrid since March 23, 1808, they had gone too far this time. The citizens of Madrid expressed their feelings quite strongly via a violent revolt on May 2, 1808. People referred to it as the Dos de Mayo Uprising or the Battle of Madrid, and it became part of the Peninsular War too.

A large crowd surrounded the royal palace, planning to physically prevent the French from taking away the children of the Royal Family. When Murat came to know of this, he sent a grenadier battalion of the Imperial Guard towards the palace. A battery of artillery accompanied this battalion. These troops would see that a clear pathway opened up for the royal departure. Murat's troops did not even appeal for peace but instead began immediately using their guns on the crowd. Naturally, the protests turned into outright rebellion immediately. As a result, the French cavalry moved through the streets of Madrid, ruthlessly putting down protestors with their sabers. The punishment continued the next day too. The French simply shot those believed to be carrying firearms. They even killed those who were not.

Murat and his fellow commanders concluded that these exemplary punishments would suffice to stop any kind of uprising in future too. The cruel suppression during the Dos de Mayo Uprising served to act as a fuse for nationwide protests against French rule. At the end of it all, the French had suffered the loss of just about 150 men. Some suffered wounds, while others died. Madrid, on the other hand, lost 500 of its citizens on that day. The French executed over a hundred of this number on May 3.

As mentioned earlier, Napoleon wanted his brother Joseph to become the next King of Spain. However, as the people of Spain received news about their monarch's imprisonment, they openly declared that they would not accept Joseph as a replacement king. The news traveled to New Spain (present Mexico) too, which was comprised of Spanish colonies. Instead, a rebel government began to operate out of Cadiz, in the name of Ferdinand VII.

Joseph accepted his kingship reluctantly, for he had no real desire to rule over Spain. His official title was King of Spain and the Indies. The Indies referred to the territories under Spanish control, beyond its local boundaries. These territories included the colonies located in the Americas. Once Napoleon placed him on the throne on June 6, 1808, Joseph went out of his way to win Spanish hearts. He strove to learn the Spanish language and attended bullfights. He made sure that the French troops remained disciplined and fair in their actions. He even professed deep devotion to the Catholic Church. However, despite all his efforts to woo them, the people of Spain refused to accept Joseph as their king. Only the Spanish aristocrats officially recognized Joseph's kingship. In August 1808, the Spanish populace drove Joseph, who had been on the throne for only three months, out of the capital city.

Joseph pleaded with Napoleon, requesting permission to return to Naples. He had always been comfortable there and felt that he had been an effective ruler. Napoleon refused to listen to his pleas. Instead, he sent more troops to Spain to ensure that Joseph returned to power. Joseph occupied the throne once more but found that his control over the people remained almost nonexistent in nature. In fact, a guerrilla war was in the offing when Venezuela declared its independence in 1810. Such events only increased Joseph's appetite for abdication! In fact, he abdicated the Spanish throne four times, over the course of two years.

Battle of Medina Del Rio Seco (July 14, 1808)

The Spanish General Cuesta's troops were determined to continue the war though Cuesta's army was small. However, he was able to gain help from the Junta of Galicia's representative assembly. He suggested that they send along their much larger army, commanded by General Joachim Blake, to support his own army. The forces combined at Villapando on July 10. There, Cuesta took charge of the combined forces. He planned to destroy the communication lines between France and Madrid. Unfortunately for the Spaniards, Napoleon was able to guess their every move. He sent reinforcements to support the French commander, Marshal Bessieres, who was in the northeastern region of Spain. This helped Bessieres to take charge of 14,000 men. Feeling that this strength was sufficient to tackle the Spaniards, he urged his troops towards Cuesta's forces. General Lasalle and his cavalry discovered the Spanish outposts near Medina Del Rios Seco on July 13.

Despite not having all his troops concentrated in one place, Cuesta still controlled a large force. There were 6,000 infantry and 550 cavalry in his army.

Blake's army was comprised of 15,000 infantry, 150 cavalry and twenty guns. Thus, the combined forces were confident that they could defeat the smaller French Army easily. However, Cuesta made a huge mistake. He selected a gentle hillside, in perfect view of the town of Medina Del Rio Seco, to position his troops. Then, he divided his army into two groups. General Blake and his troops remained in the southeast, along with the vanguard bridge. They occupied the plateau of Valdecuevas on a prominent hill. Cuesta, along with his Army of Castile and a division from the army of Galicia, stationed themselves a mile away, just to the left and behind Blake's group. The two armies could not see each other at all. Historians have debated the reasoning behind the implementation of such impractical measures, but no one has been able to come up with a valid answer yet. Maybe Cuesta hoped that Blake would have to retreat, thereby leaving him as the hero who saved the day.

It took Bessieres just a few minutes to comprehend how vulnerable the Spaniards were, while advancing towards them on July 14, 1808. The mile-long gap in the center of the Spanish line sufficed to give French a superb advantage. General Mouton and his five battalions prevented Cuesta and his troops from moving anywhere. Then, the French focused on outflanking Blake's troops with the aid of fifteen battalions. Generals Merle and Sabathier were in charge. When the fighting had been going on for an hour or so, Bessieres ordered Lasalle's cavalry to fill in a gap and attack Blake's unguarded flank. Soon enough, Blake's entire army began to withdraw from the battlefield. Only one battalion from Navarre stood its ground, forming a square, in order to confront the French. This battalion helped Blake to escape successfully. Cuesta, who should have been retreating too, commanded his Galician division to attack Bessieres' army as soon as it appeared on the hill. The gallant forces managed to cut through the French lines in the center and captured four guns. However, they could not withstand the French might for long and had to retreat. Furthermore, their losses were heavy. Completely cowed, Cuesta ordered his troops to move back through the town of Medina Del Rio Seco.

Bessieres knew that his army had been marching and battling since 2:00 a.m. Therefore, he did not force his soldiers to pursue the Spaniards. Regardless, the Army of Galicia suffered 3,000 casualties. Around 400 men died, while 500 suffered grievous wounds. The French took 1,200 prisoners. The remaining soldiers deserted the army. The Army of Castile suffered just 155 casualties. Around 105 French soldiers died, while 300 sustained wounds. Nevertheless, the defeat sufficed to halt any more Spanish threats to the

French lines of communication. Joseph Bonaparte could travel to Madrid safely and take over the throne on July 20, 1808.

Napoleon wanted Dupont to take over Andalusia. However, the overly optimistic Napoleon had provided him with forces which were insufficient in both number and quality to complete the task. Dupont's troops had to move back towards the River Guadalquivir's valley. Soon enough, Vedel arrived with his troops. Dupont waited, not wishing to proceed towards the north via the mountain passes. It would be akin to abandoning Andalusia. Yet he wondered if he could remain there for long, or even launch an attack on an enemy.

Unlike him, the Spaniards were not willing to wait. They brought together the forces of Andalusia (Castanos), the army from Grenada (Reding) and diverse bands of popular irregulars for launching an assault. The combined forces totaled 23,000 men and thirty guns. General Reding was in command. In contrast, General Dupont had just about 14,000 men with him and forty guns. Dupont positioned his troops along the northern bank of the River Guadalquivir. They were a little ways away from eastern Andujar. Dupont's main army waited at Andujar. Vedel's division remained in the east, focusing on the river line, as well as the line of communications that stretched northeast through the towns of La Carolina and Baylen, as well as the Sierra Morena passes.

As per the Spanish strategy, Castanos would keep Dupont at Andujar, giving General Reding sufficient time to flank him upstream. Reding's troops would cross the river and land on the French left rear. Unfortunately for them, the plan did not work out well. The Spaniards made mistakes due to their own confusion. However, the French made worse mistakes. For instance, Vedel's troops had moved away to La Carolina, believing a threat to be present there. As a result, Reding was able to take over Baylen without engaging in a fight with the French. Unaware of what had taken place, Dupont left Andujar and marched with his troops to Baylen. He had a weak advance guard with him. The center of his column carried along the wounded, as well as the accumulated loot. The rearguard, however, was strong, good enough to repulse attacks from the Castanos.

When Dupont's advance guard reached Baylen on July 19, they noticed the presence of Reding's troops there. By the time the French arrived, Reding had deployed his army across the road into town. He had also kept a group on standby for delaying Vedel if he were to arrive there. Thus, the Spanish displayed better organization in contrast to Dupont and his troops, who were tired and unable to engage in battle. Dupont attempted several piecemeal attacks, rather than a good, long fight. As a result, the French troops lost their confidence completely. In fact, they refused to make any further efforts at all. Realizing that two Spanish armies had trapped his troops and that the French Army was beginning to disintegrate, Dupont sued for peace terms. By this time, Vedel had also arrived. However, using Dupont's 20,000 men as hostages, the Spanish army applied pressure on him. Reding had to order Vedel to surrender his entire army. The Spanish suffered around 1,000 casualties. Thus, the entire French Corps suffered defeat on July 22, 1808.

Negotiations, however, continued until July 23, when the French surrendered completely. Around 17,635 had remained uninjured. Baylen was sufficient to loosen France's hold on Spain and the French Army had to withdraw to the north of Elbro. Europeans began to wonder if the label of invincibility that had followed the French Army everywhere was actually true! The reputation of the French armies took a severe beating. Dupont lost his titles and had to face public disgrace. He even suffered two years in prison. Napoleon had to intervene in the Peninsular War personally, to see if he could restore France's reputation.

Great Britain's Sir Arthur Wellesley was also jubilant about his Anglo-Portuguese army's victory over the French forces near the village of Rolica in Portugal on August 17, 1808. Wellesley did not want reinforcements arriving at the mouth of the River Maceira, which lay to the west of Vimeiro, in order to launch a counterattack. However, Junot had already left Lisbon on the night of August 15. He brought together the divisions of Loison and Delaborde at Torres Vedras first, prior to marching towards Vimeiro on the night of August 20. Wellesley's army was vigilant that night. His troops were concentrated on a ridge that stretched westwards from the village of Vimeiro, before heading towards the sea. The British left positioned itself on the hill in front of the village, and this marked the beginning of Battle of Vimeiro in August 1808.

Around 9:00 a.m. on August 21, Wellesley spied Junot's army even amidst the clouds of dust that rose towards the sky. The army was moving towards the east of Vimeiro, in order to attack the British left flank. The commander had sufficient time to urge his troops to abandon the western ridge, and instead, move to another one. This ridge lay northeast of Vimeiro and passed through Ventosa. As a result, Junot had to attempt a divided attack. His main force would fight the troops on Vimeiro Hill, while Brennier's brigade would have to move northwards if they wished to attack the British left. When he saw the British army on Ventosa Ridge,

Junot sent Solignac and his troops towards the north, such that they could help Brennier.

The French Army began the attack on Vimeiro Hill. Thomieres and Charlot, with their respective brigades, advanced in columns. Their approach remained screened by tirailleurs. As a result, the British forces in the front, who were engaging in continual skirmishes, had to retreat from the foot of the hill. However, the French forces were in for a surprise! Fane's Sixth and Anstruther's Seventh brigades, which were part of the British infantry, began firing at the French troops. The French found themselves reeling under the heavy attack. However, Junot refused to let this setback reduce the morale of his troops. He sent two battalions of grenadiers, under the command of St. Clair, to battle the midpoint of the British line on Vimeiro Hill. This time, too, the British infantry handled the attack efficiently. They converged on the French column from all three sides. A desperate Junot sent the remaining battalions of grenadiers, under the command of Maransin, towards Vimeiro village. However, Wellesley had instructed four companies, belonging to Acland's Eighth Brigade, to come down from Ventosa Ridge. These companies surrounded Maransin's troops. The close-range battle on the streets of the village was so vicious that the French grenadiers decided to withdraw.

When all the action on Vimeiro Hill was ending, Solignac and Brennier encountered the British forces at Ventosa. Their respective brigades had to move northwards, since there was a ravine that ran under the ridge. As a result, Solignac and Brennier lost contact with one another. Solignac had asked his troops to climb the slope lying below Ventosa. Brennier just kept pushing northwards, hoping to find an easier route to handle. When Solignac and his brigade reached the crest of the ridge, Ferguson's Second Brigade and Nightingall's Third Brigade were waiting to receive them with musketry fire. Confused, the French broke their ranks, prior to fleeing from the advancing British lines. By then, Brennier had arrived on the scene. He had the advantage for some time but eventually had to fall back too.

By midday, it was all over, leaving the French with 2,000 casualties. The British-Portuguese army suffered 720 casualties and the French lost thirteen of their guns. Soon after, the British-Portuguese army had the advantage of advancing upon French-occupied Lisbon. However, the next in command, Sir Henry Burrard, was rather overcautious by nature, and not at all as adventurous as Wellesley was.

Napoleon Enters Madrid (December 4, 1808)

After overcoming Spanish resistance at Somosierra Pass on November 30, the French troops took up a position outside the gates of Madrid on December 1, 1808.

The local populace found it hard to defend Madrid, with its lack of narrow and winding streets. There were no fortifications in sight. The gates were purely ornamental affairs, which were in place to make it easy for collecting duties. Even the hill Retiro, which overlooked the city, had little to offer in the way of protection. Only about 3,000 Spanish soldiers remained in the city to defend it. The majority of them were new recruits, who seemed to have arrived in the city at the same time that the French did. However, the population of Madrid believed that they could defend their city against any kind of invaders merely through enthusiasm and some sort of weaponry. After all, their Spanish heroes had overcome the first siege of Saragossa with great success. Thus, when the French appeared at their gates, around 20,000 people picked up some kind of weapon or the other for attacking the alien soldiers. They even constructed a massive wall around Madrid, with the help of paving slabs. They were not to know that when the French bombarded the city, the chips from these slabs would cause immense damage. However, no one made an effort to fortify the crucial Retiro heights.

The French Army was waiting for Napoleon to arrive, and arrive he did, on December 2. The French Emperor hoped that the people would not put up much of a fight and would surrender quickly. However, the Junta refused to give in to his demands, even when he mentioned the French victory at Austerlitz. According to the Junta, the population of Madrid would rather bury itself under the ruins of houses, rather than allow French invaders to enter the city. Therefore, the French began to prepare for an invasion of Madrid on the nights of December 2 and 3. Towards this end, the French Army placed gun batteries in front of the eastern and northern gates of the city. It also prepared to focus the main attack against Retiro Hill. Despite everything, Napoleon wanted to enter Madrid without engaging in warfare. However, the Spaniards turned down his demand for the second time on the morning of December 3. In fact, a commander of the Spanish defending forces, Captain-General Castelar, suggested a truce for twelve hours. He wanted to give the field armies that were approaching Madrid time to reach the city. However, Napoleon was in no mood to listen and decided that France would attack.

Villatte's Division of Victor's Corps waited for the French artillery to create some breaches in the weak defenses that the Spaniards had set up in the area. Then he launched the initial assault against the Retiro. The defenders of the hill could not withstand the might of the French forces and were soon running away from their positions. The French pursued them into the very heart of Madrid. Then, they captured three of the gates, prior to initiating an attack on the palace of the Duke of Medina Celi. Napoleon then asked his forces to halt their actions. He placed a request for peaceful surrender, a third time. The local populace wanted to continue their defensive actions. The military leaders, however, were well aware of how vulnerable their position was, especially as the French artillery had reached the top of Retiro Hill. Therefore, they were ready to surrender.

Another commander of the defending forces of Madrid, General Morla, appeared before Napoleon, wishing to begin negotiations. Napoleon treated him to a string of abuses, thereby lowering his enthusiasm for fighting even further. Towards the end, Napoleon issued a strong threat. The city had until 6:00 a.m., on December 4, 1808, to surrender. In case Madrid refused, the French forces would kill every individual found under arms. The frightened Junta decided that it would be best to surrender. It was not so easy to convince the people of Madrid to drop their weapons. However, the speed with which certain events occurred proved to be of great help. Since the French blockade was not yet complete, several thousand citizens managed to escape from the city. Thereafter, the Junta documented a capitulation agreement. The Junta sent this agreement to Napoleon, who agreed to all eleven articles. He would not adhere to them, however, once he took control of Madrid. Napoleon re-entered Madrid in triumph on December 4. Unlike his usual wont, Napoleon did not promptly sack the city. This was because he was saving it for his older brother, Joseph, or rather, King Joseph.

Although the defense of Madrid had not lasted very long, it had a dramatic impact on the fighting in Spain. For instance, General Sir John Moore of the British army resident in Portugal, was debating whether he should remain in Spain or not when he heard reports about Napoleon being stuck outside Madrid. Of course, the rumor was false, but the commander was not to know that. He felt that the time was ripe to launch an assault on Marshal Soult's troops located around Burgos. He hopes that this threat to the French communication lines would prompt Napoleon to abandon Madrid. To Moore's delight, Napoleon did set aside his plans for invading Portugal, upon learning of Moore's actions, and set off instead in pursuit of Moore. However, when he discovered that Moore and his troops had failed to fall into his trap, Napoleon abandoned the chase to Soult and returned to Madrid. This was his first and last visit to Spain.

Great Britain's Army, under the command of Lieutenant General Sir John Moore, had been striving to escape the pursuing French for quite some time. The land forces moved through Castile and Galacia, before reaching the sea finally. Here, at Corunna, they rendezvoused with an evacuation fleet. However, Moore needed some time to embark his forces. Therefore, he decided to attack the French at a place called Monte Mero. This hill lay just a few miles down the main road on the south side from Corunna. Moore's forces stretched from east to west. In other words, it stretched from a point that lay north of Piedralonga village to a point north of Elvina village, in Spain. Thus began the Battle of Corunna.

The British were confident of victory, for Moore positioned various groups under diverse leaders with great thought and wisdom. For instance, Hope had a wonderfully strong three-brigade division in place on the eastern side of the line and Biard's equally strong three-brigade division lay in place on the western side of the line. Nonetheless, there were some disadvantages too. For instance, their position was low in comparison to the Heights of Penasquedo. Then again, cannonballs would have to travel a long distance for hitting targets to the south. The open right flank positioned in the eastern region around Elvina seemed to be rather weak in nature. Moore could hardly do anything about the first issue. With regard to the second and third ones, he ensured that two weak divisions remained behind his right flank. One of them was Paget's group, while the other was Fraser's. Both would remain out of sight of the approaching French Army.

The French were around 16,000 in number. Their commander was Marshal Soult. The army had forty guns in its possession. The marshal placed Delaborde's division on the eastern side of the line and Merle's group on the western side of it. He hoped that they would keep the British engaged in the very same place, without letting them move. Meanwhile, Mermet's men flanking the left of Soult's forces would launch an assault on Biard's group. These men would receive assistance from the cavalry divisions under the command of La Houssaye and Franceschi. As for Soult himself, he took his own group to the south of the British forces on the Heights of Penasquedo. He would receive assistance from Lorge's cavalry.

The battle that commenced on January 16, 1809, was an extremely bitter one. It took place in and around Elvina. Despite losing both Moore and

Baird, the British forces managed to remain in control. For instance, Paget's troops prevented both Mermet's division and La Houssaye's cavalry from gaining an upper hand. Similarly, Fraser's group tackled Franceschi's cavalry successfully. Thus, in tactical terms, the British won the Battle of Corunna. They managed to leave in the night, despite not being in the same condition as they had been prior to the commencement of the battle. They had lost around 900 men, while the French lost around 1,500 soldiers. It was commendable that the British forces had stood up to large numbers of some of the best soldiers in the whole of Europe and their experienced leaders without flinching. True, they had to leave Spain, but by distracting Napoleon's Army at a critical juncture in European politics, the British had prevented the French Emperor from taking over the entire nation of Spain. The battle also served to give the Spanish revolt some more time for gathering its strength. Napoleon himself left Spain and returned to France on January 17, 1809.

The Wars of the Fifth Coalition

From April onwards began the wars of the Fifth Coalition. This time around, there were only two members—Austria and Great Britain. The partnership lasted through October 1809. Both parties were suffering due to the imposition of

Napoleon's Continental System. Therefore, when Austria witnessed a large number of French troops entering Spain, it sensed an opportunity to launch a campaign against Napoleon's rule.

The reason for France sending troops to Spain was the rise in Spanish rebellions against the presence of the French in the country. Vowing to liberate as many nations as possible from French rule, the Austrians decided that a large-scale revolution throughout the Confederation of the Rhine was essential. Towards this end, their troops invaded Bavaria on April 9, indicating that they had begun a war of German liberation. However, the Bavarians were inclined to favor Napoleon, since they had benefitted from Austria's defeat at the hands of the French Army earlier. They refused to take the side of the Austrians. Instead, they rallied around Napoleon as he gathered his troops and made them ready for battle. A thrilled Napoleon declared that if Austria desired to be slapped, he was all for it! He also threatened the Emperor of Austria that if he dared to engage in any hostile moves against the French, his reign would soon end.

Marshal Louis-Nicolas Davout's III Corps deployed south of Ratisbon in Bavaria. However, its positioning was such that the corps was in great danger of becoming isolated from the rest of the French Army. All this had happened due to a misunderstanding of the orders that had come from the top. Davout figured out his mistake and strove to figure out a way of saving his troops. He had to look after approximately 47,000 men or so. Unfortunately, Archduke Charles of Austria had also figured out what was happening. The only snag was that he did not know where, exactly, Davout was, or where his troops planned to move. In actuality, Davout had decided that he might as well take his troops towards Abensburg, where he could link up with Bavarian Lefebvre and his VI Corps. However, his troops would have to march along the southern bank of the River Danube, in order to reach the selected place. Accordingly, his army set off on April 19. Davout had divided his III Corps into four columns. He had sent his vulnerable trains ahead via the good road moving parallel to the river. The cavalry and infantry found it easy to tackle the poorer forest roads that lay inland. It helped that Davout and his men were quick in their movements.

Archduke Charles, along with his 80,000-strong army, decided to begin his search for Davout on April 19, 1809. However, his men were not as speedy in their movements as the French were. Then again, not knowing where exactly he could catch up with Davout, Charles spread his men wide, ensuring that all corps would converge on Ratisbon from the south. Whether by luck, or by intuition, Charles almost caught up with Davout. The Austrian

III, or the westernmost corps, under the command of General Hohenzollern, came upon Davout's rear flank on a route that lay between the villages of Teugn and Hausen. The French were making their way through the narrow defile that lay between Saale and Abbach on the River Danube. This rear flank was under the command of General Saint-Hillaire. Even the cavalry was present, under the command of Montbrun and Friant. This cavalry attacked the Austrians with great ferocity in the wooded terrain. Hohenzollern could only offer piecemeal skirmishes in exchange. Soon enough, the French experts outfought his troops successfully. The losses were heavy on both sides, with the Austrians losing around 3,800 men and the French losing around 4,500.

The Austrians failed to receive adequate support from Archduke Charles. The archduke could not figure out where the main weight of Davout's Corps was and failed to realize that the fighting taking place along a considerable length of his front deserved help too. Since he missed his chance, the French trains and the bulk of the French III Corps managed to link up successfully, and without mishap, with the rest of the French Army. The outcome would have been different if Archduke Charles had urged his troops to move speedily towards the road along the River Danube and position themselves there prior to Davout's arrival.

Alternatively, he could have recognized that the action occurring at Teugn-Hausen meant that the bulk of Davout's Corps was nearby and laid a trap. Charles had a numerical advantage. If Davout had found his supply lines cut, he would have been at a disadvantage. A severe drubbing would have sufficed to bring down the morale of the French Army! Thus, Charles missed his best chance of beating the French at their game at Teugn-Hausen.

After what happened on April 19, Archduke Charles divided his army into two wings. Charles took charge of the right wing, which positioned itself to the south of the River Danube, stretching from west to east. While Hohenzollern and his III Corps remained around Hausen, the IV Corps moved towards Dunzling in the east. The one Reserve Corps, under the command of Liechtenstein, was stationed on the road north from Eggmuhl. With regard to the right wing, Hiller took command, stationing them towards the southwest. V Corps, under the command of Ludwig and II Reserve Corps, under the command of Kienmayer, positioned itself east of the River Abens. This was just about 20 miles to the southwest of Hausen. Hiller remained at Mainburg towards the south. Finally, two corps covered the northern region of the River Danube. The Austrians numbered 161,000.

Napoleon had kept himself informed about all the Austrian movements. However, he was unaware of the presence of Austrians near Dunzling and Eggmuhl. Nonetheless, he decided to spread out his army of 113,000 soldiers. While Lannes had charge of a strong provisional corps for launching the main attack, Davout positioned his troops on the left. The troops were to focus on Teugu. Lefebvre's VII Corps remained around Abensburg, with Vandamme's VIII Corps not too far away. A small garrison protected Ratisbon and the bridge over the River Danube. Massena's IV Corps and Quidnot's II Corps remained further to the right.

One would have thought that with such careful planning, the Austrians would come out the victors. However, this was not to be. Lannes began the assault on April 20, 1809, as he urged his forces towards Bachl on the southeast. France's allies, the First Bavarian Division, were also moving east, pushing Austrian forces, under the command of Thierry, out of Offenstetten. While Thierry's troops attempted to reach Bachl, they ran into the light cavalry of the French Army. Sensing a collapse, the Austrians began to retreat further southeast. Lannes pursued them, until they had to leave Rohr and move towards the River Grosse Laaber. While they were retreating, Lannes' troops moved towards the same river, albeit at Rottenburg. There, he linked up with Hiller's Corps, which had arrived earlier in the day. The French and Austrians engaged in a clash, wherein Hiller's defensive tactics won the day. When it became dark, Hiller urged his troops to retreat towards Landshut. He had abandoned the battle.

On the other side, the Second Bavarian Division, which was moving to the right of Lannes' Corps, took on the Austrians, under the command of Bianchi. This division had crossed the River Abens at Biburg. For a couple of hours or so, the Bavarians were not able to make any progress, as the Austrians were determined to hold on to their positions. Neither Lannes, nor the Third Bavarian Division, who were too far ahead, could offer support to the Second Bavarian Division. Therefore, Napoleon sent his Wurttemberg troops forwards. This sufficed to convince the Austrians that they had better retreat. Thus, Bianchi's troops and Radetzky's troops moved to Pfeffenhausen near the River Laaber.

Napoleon was not about to let the Austrians go unharmed. He ordered the Second Bavarian Division to attack the Austrians at Pfeffenhausen at night. The Austrians were unprepared for an assault in the night. They decided to retreat to Landshut. Thus, the Bavarians managed to cross the burning bridge at Laaber and take over the village during the chaos. At the end of it all, the Austrians on the left were in retreat and the French had control over Laaber. As for Archduke Charles and his troops on the right, he found himself completely isolated in the north. While the Austrians suffered over 7,000 casualties, the French suffered around 1,000, over the course of two days. Regardless, the Austrians did gain something from this battle. The French garrison at Ratisbon surrendered on April 20. Additionally, Charles gained control over the strong bridge spanning the River Danube, permitting his troops to escape across the river. Above all, Napoleon remained unaware about the whereabouts of the main Austrian Army, which was the right wing.

The French wanted to complete the annihilation of the left wing of the Austrian forces. Therefore, they engaged in the Battle of Landshut on April 21, 1809. At the end of the previous day's battle, Field Marshal Lieutenant Johann Freiherr von Hiller found himself taking shelter at Landshut. Archduke Charles and his troops, on the other hand, remained at Ratisbon. Napoleon continued to believe that Hiller was in command of the main Austrian force. Therefore, he decided to take the main French Army towards Landshut. Believing that the right wing was a small one, Napoleon left Davout behind to deal with these Austrian troops whenever they appeared before the French.

Vandamme's cavalry was the first to engage Hiller's troops in battle, as soon as the French reached Landshut, which was located on the southern bank of the River Isar. It linked to the northern bank via two bridges. One of the bridges connected to the suburb of Zwischen den Brucken, where Austrian troops were in position. While the terrible cavalry battle between the two armies was taking place on the plains that were to the north of the River Isar, Lannes' infantry units decided to attack the Austrians at Zwischen den Brucken. However, before the assault could spread to the connecting bridge between Landshut and Zwischen den Brucken, the Austrians withdrew. They were not completely successful in setting the bridge on fire, since the weather was wet. Therefore, the French were able to capture the majority of the Austrians.

By this time, Napoleon and his troops had arrived near Landshut. Without a single moment's delay, he ordered General Georges Mouton to take his grenadiers and invade the Bavarian town. Mouton's men moved across the smoldering bridge without fear, muskets in hand. They broke the main gate and entered the town. Group after group followed Mouton. As a result, Landshut came under French control by 1:00 p.m. When Massena's Corps finally arrived at Landshut, the town was already in French hands. The left wing of the Austrians had already beaten a retreat. They had to leave their supplies behind, towards the north of the river, which benefitted the French wonderfully well!

While setting up camp around Landshut after the battle with the Austrians, Napoleon realized that they had not connected with the main part of the Austrian army at all. All the while, he had been thinking that the French had defeated the main army at Abensburg and then driven them through Landshut. Due to this misunderstanding, Davout's Corps found itself confronting three intact corps, under the command of Archduke Charles, for the second time. Davout's forces had positioned themselves further north. On his part, the archduke had made a mistake about judging the enemy's positions. Charles had felt that Davout's forces constituted the main army of the French. Therefore, he'd decided that he would go in for a decisive battle on April 22, 1809. This was known as the Battle of Eckmuhl.

The archduke had made his plans. His forces would challenge Davout's army, which had positioned itself in an area that lay south of Abbach on the River Danube. However, his troops would have to travel quite some distance to reach the place. As a result, there was a delay in launching an assault at the planned time. Meanwhile, Davout had sent an emissary to Napoleon. The emissary contacted Napoleon in the early hours of April 22. He convinced the emperor that Davout's forces were in great danger. Napoleon arranged for reinforcements immediately. He also planned to take his main army north from Landshut, thereby annihilating the main forces under the command of Archduke Charles.

Charles had deployed his forces in a line that stretched roughly towards both, the north and south. The south flank positioned itself at Eckmuhl. The Austrian Army's northern part comprised of the strongest soldiers. Charles hoped that these troops would be able to flank the French Army in this region. He didn't know that Napoleon would tackle the weak southern flank first, while Davout kept the others busy in the front. Lannes moved first, along with a group of strong provisional corps. He would begin the attack. Napoleon followed him, along with Massena's Corps.

Around seven or eight in the morning, the cavalries on both sides clashed. Rosenburg, who was in charge of the Austrian IV Corps belonging to the south flank, came to know of the attack around midmorning. By midday, he realized that his troops were about to confront a major attack from the south. Immediately, he sent warning signals to Charles. The archduke received the message between one and two in the afternoon when he was just about to launch an offensive against Davout's forces. Caught off guard completely, Charles decided that his troops had best beat a retreat to Ratisbon. He passed along the message to the majority of his forces. He instructed Rosenburg to take up the role of rearguard for the whole army. There was no way to help him. He was on his own.

A helpless Rosenburg had 18,000 soldiers with him. They were part of the IV Corps and the III Corps. They would have to face Napoleon's huge army of 90,000. The French arrived there at 3:00 p.m. and began their assault immediately. Within an hour, they had taken Eckmuhl. Yet they did not stop their advance, merely widening it as they went along. The Austrians put up a good fight wherever they could, despite some having to sacrifice their lives and some having to give themselves up as prisoners of war. They withdrew in good order, despite the huge challenge. As if this was not enough, the Austrian cavalry had to suffer a huge defeat at Alteglofsheim, just a few hours before darkness descended on the battle scene. However, the defeat prevented the French cavalry from interfering with the rest of the Austrian forces' retreat. At the end of the day, the Austrians, who were camped to the south of Ratisbon, felt mauled, disorganized, dispirited and defeated. However, they refused to feel routed, as their army was largely intact. They had lost around 12,000 men, while the French had lost 6,000.

During the early hours of the morning, Charles and his army crossed the River Danube successfully via the Ratisbon Bridge and a self-constructed pontoon bridge. Thus, Napoleon was not able to break the main Austrian Army as he had hoped to. Instead, he had defeated Austria's invasion of Bavaria. Additionally, he had managed to divide their forces during the battle, preventing them from withstanding the might of the French center. Nonetheless, the fighting would continue, since the Austrian armies stationed in Germany were still in good shape and eager to confront the French Army in the days to come.

The Battle of Oporto on May 12, 1809, was a confrontation between the 18,000-strong British-Portuguese army and the 11,000-strong French Army. The former was under the command of General Arthur Wellesley, while the latter was under the command of Marshal Soult. Strangely, even though the French forces outnumbered the combined forces of the British and Portuguese in the peninsula, they often faced defeat at the hands of their enemies. This was because they had to cope with numerous Spanish uprisings and other hostile populations in the French-controlled territories across Europe. As a result, the French Army often found itself dispersed in various directions and barely concentrated in one area. Additionally, the different French Corps failed to remain communicative with each other. Therefore, at the most critical of times, they failed to provide adequate support to one another.

When this battle took place on May 12, 1809, Soult had been in his headquarters at Oporto. Half his corps had stayed with him, while the remaining corpsmen had scattered themselves across the countryside. They strove to keep the lines of communication open, as well as find routes for a potential retreat if and when it was needed. Since Soult and his corps were occupying Portuguese territory, Wellesley decided that the time was ripe for an attack on the French forces. Although Wellesley tried his best to keep the attack a surprise, Soult received warning of it a day in advance. Immediately, he planned his withdrawal. He took his forces along with him to the north of the River Douro. He wished to destroy the bridge leading to Oporto. He also wanted to sink all the boats present there, or at least tow them to the north side of the river.

Soult feared an attack from the River Douro's wide estuary or from the sea. Therefore, he positioned his forces in Oporto and to the west, to keep a keen watch. He discarded the possibility of an attack from the east and had it poorly watched. Soult felt that the British would take a few days to organize a river crossing of a large number of troops. He was quite reasonable in his deduction, for it did take time to set up a river crossing. However, Soult had failed to take into consideration that Wellesley was very innovative in his strategies. He never failed to take the initiative. Furthermore, the local populace was always eager to help the British. In fact, a local barber helped the British to reach the northern side of River Douro via a few unguarded barges that were lying upstream. Wellesley was thrilled when he realized how perfect the location was for positioning his artillery! Furthermore, the high ground on the south bank concealed his location from anyone who was approaching from downstream. Above all, there was a highly defensible seminary on the north bank. Wellesley put Paget in command of those troops that would try to cross and hold the seminary. Sherbrooke took charge of the troops that would cover the riverbank facing the city of Oporto. Finally, Wellesley ordered Murray to take along a few battalions across the river, albeit a few miles upstream, and create a diversion for Soult's forces.

Paget's troops began crossing the river to reach the seminary at 10:00 a.m. The French took notice only half an hour later, by which time several hundred men had already crossed and positioned themselves. They had the support of the artillery on the opposite bank too. Therefore, it was easy to counter the French assaults. Paget received serious injuries, forcing him to hand over the command to

Hill. However, the British suffered fewer losses in comparison to the French. Soon, Soult decided to pull his troops out of the city and attack the British forces. However, some part of the populace rioted. The rest of the populace began to help Sherbrooke and his troops cross the river by providing their own boats. By midafternoon, the French forces were in full retreat towards the northeast. Murray and his forces, who were watching the retreat, did not think of interfering and destroying the French forces. They had also noticed the French's rough handling of some British dragoons, who had dared to interfere with the retreating soldiers!

While the British lost 123 men, the French lost 600. Around 1,500 wounded soldiers were admitted to hospitals at Oporto. The French also lost six of their own guns and fifty-two siege guns that had originally belonged to the Portuguese. Those of the French who managed to retreat successfully moved on to Galicia. However, they lost their baggage and guns along the way. Thus, Portugal remained free from French invaders for some time at least.

Napoleon had always wanted to take the control over Vienna and, finally, it happened in mid-May 1809. He wanted to cross the River Danube and reach the north bank, for somewhere around that area, he would find Archduke Charles and the main Austrian army. If he could defeat this army in battle, he could end the French campaign. However, the Austrians were keeping a keen watch on all the normal crossing places, forcing Napoleon to seek alternatives. Therefore, he narrowed his choice to a location that lay slightly to the east of Vienna. Here, the River Danube was slow and wide. Additionally, Lobau, a large, wooded island, lay close to the northern bank. This could prove to be a secure staging ground for the French. Towards this end, Napoleon placed an advance guard on the island on May 19. The French began setting up a bridge to Lobau, which they completed by midday on May 20. Massena and his IV Corps were the first to cross. Opposite Lobau, on the northern bank of the river, there were two villages—the smaller Essling and the larger Aspern. The walls of the houses were made of stone. Walls made from stones and ditches surrounded the villages. Essling revealed a granary that had thick walls on its northern side. Aspern had a walled cemetery and a church. A ditch and a road sufficed to connect the villages. The French decided that the buildings in both villages would prove to be good strong points.

Unfortunately for the French, the makeshift bridge over the Danube broke on the night of May 20. Nonetheless, at least three or four of Massena's infantry divisions had managed to cross the river by the morning of May 21, by the time the French had finished repairing the bridge. Napoleon sent Molitor and his troops to hold Aspern, with the aid of Legrand and his group. Massena's focus was on Aspern. Boudet and his group took over Essling. Marshal Lannes would lend adequate support. The French cavalry, comprised of Lasalle's Light Cavalry Division, guarded the area between both the villages. They had arrived the previous day. D'Espagne's Heavy Cavalry Division and Marulaz's Light Cavalry Division had crossed the newly repaired bridge early in the morning. Napoleon wanted the bridge in place to pursue a retreating enemy.

The Austrian Army had been marching through the night in order to reach the French bridgehead. They had planned to use four corps converging on the French in the form of five huge columns. The French noticed the attacking columns of Austria early afternoon of May 21. However, serious assaults began only at 3:00 p.m. The Austrians had taken over both the cemetery and the church of Aspern, along with a major portion of the village, by 4:30 p.m. Molitar lost almost half his men. The situation improved only after the arrival of Legrand's division in the form of reinforcements. Thereafter, the village of Aspern kept changing hands, as if it were a seesaw! Only when Saint-Cyr arrived with Massena's fourth division did the situation stabilize. The French had some part of

Aspern under their control. The Austrians controlled the rest of the village.

The French were unable to access healthy reinforcements during the day, due to the bridge breaking every so often. Then, on the nights of May 20 and May 21, they managed to help the French Guard, as well as three infantry divisions belonging to the II Corps, across. This sufficed to increase the strength of the infantry. Napoleon even planned to send the III Corps across, as soon as there was enough room for such a maneuver. When the fighting began once again, around 4:00 a.m. on May 22, 1809, it was vicious and intense. By 7:00 a.m., the French had control over both the villages. Lannes' II Corps was comprised of three divisions that launched an attack on the Austrian center. The Austrians possessed superior artillery. Therefore, they managed to stall Lannes' assault until 9:00 a.m. The French's manmade bridge broke again. Therefore, Napoleon could not send across any reinforcements.

By midday, the Austrians had pushed the French back, wherein they concentrated between Essling and Aspern. Around 1:00 p.m., Aspern was back in Austrian hands. Even the Young Guard could not stop them. The Austrians even managed to wrest Essling away from the French by 3:00 p.m. However, a counterattack by the Young Guard sufficed to push them back. By this time, both armies decided that they had had enough of battle. While Napoleon began organizing a retreat to Lobau, Archduke Charles decided to give the French a parting shot in the form of massive artillery bombardment.

The Austrians suffered 23,000 casualties, due to their ill-coordinated attacks on Essling. The French lost heavily, too, for their losses were equal to that of the Austrians. At the end of it all, both sides had achieved only partial success. There had been too much bloodshed on both sides, and all for nothing. As for Napoleon, the Aspern-Essling battle proved to be a setback for his political career. It became obvious that his aura of invincibility was gradually diminishing.

In the Battle of Wagram, which happened in July 1809, Napoleon's army of 180,000 men and 500 guns confronted Archduke Charles' army of 140,000 men and 450 guns. Napoleon was attempting to cross the River Danube a second time. This time, too, he decided to utilize the Island of Lobau for constructing bridges. However, he decided to opt for multiple bridges, possessing an improved design. He would also see that floating missiles did not destroy these well-protected bridges. He ensured that the French artillery improved with the aid of pieces that the French

Army had looted from Austrian stores. Finally, he created a highly strong army, comprised of Davout's III Corps, Eugene's Army of Italy, Bernadotte's IX Corps of Saxons etc. Above all, Legrand's division of Massena's Corps would create a feint, permitting Napoleon to launch an attack from the southwest corner of Lobau, instead of the northwest one.

Despite the presence of a thunderstorm and icy rain on July 4, at 11:00 p.m., the French launched an assault via their artillery. Within five minutes, they had a pre-prepared pontoon bridge in place over the final stretch of water. This helped Massena's troops to begin crossing the River Danube. His troops helped to push Nordmann's Advance Guard out of Gross Enzersdorf, which lay to the north of the main crossing, by 9:00 a.m. on July 5. Around 10:00 a.m., the Corps of Oudinot, Davout and Massena had taken up position between Wittau and Gross Enzersdorf, in order to help the remainder of the French Army to cross the River Danube. By 2:00 p.m., the French began to move west, as well as north. Massena's troops focused on the west, wherein they wrested Essling from the Austrians by 2:30 p.m. They also wrested Aspern from Klenau's VI Corps by 4:30 p.m.

Davout and Oudinot moved north towards a line on the Russbach. They positioned themselves between Markgrafneusiedl and Wagram. Bernadotte's IX

Corps and Eugene's Army of Italy rushed into the gaps opened up by the troops belonging to Oudinot and Massena. By 6:00 p.m., the French troops had positioned themselves in the form of an arc. This arc began from Aspern north to a place that lay just south of Wagram. Then, it moved east towards Markgrafneusidl. To the Austrians' surprise, Napoleon launched an attack on them late in the night. The attack took place near Wagram. However, Napoleon's late-night attacks on July 5 failed.

Archduke Charles took the initiative on July 6, 1809. Around 4:00 a.m., he sent Rosenburg's Austrian IV Corps to attack Davout's French III Corps on the French right. The attack took place near Markgrafneusidl. Although Rosenburg was successful, he lost his advantage, for the other Austrians failed to attack the French left simultaneously. Therefore, Napoleon's reserve forces sufficed to boost Davout's morale and push back Rosenburg. Regardless, Archduke Charles decided to continue with the assault on the French left flank. He instructed four corps to take over the task. From north to south, these corps included Klenau's VI Corps, Bellegarde's I Corps, Lichtenstein's Reserve Corps and Kollowrat's III Corps. Bellagarde's Corps tangled with the corps commanded by Bernadotte and Massena, over Aderklaa. He did gain an initial advantage, but

Napoleon's reserve forces rushed over and regained the village. The concern about their flanks prevented Kollowrat and Lichenstein from pushing their troops beyond a line with Bellagarde's Corps. Klenau's VI Corps had better success, while challenging Boudet's division of Massena's Corps. His troops reached Essling by 9:00 a.m. Although the Austrians pursued the French, when they came to Lobau, they met their match in the French artillery. Klenau's troops suffered badly.

Davout, who was in charge of the French right flank, began an assault on the Austrians gathered near Markgrafneusiedl, around 10:00 a.m. Klenau's Corps seemed to be the target of the whole French Army! Napoleon sent across Massena's troops, aided by cavalry and Grand Artillery battery, to attack them. Massena succeeded in driving away Klenau's troops. Davout made good progress on the French right. Thus, the climax of the battle was about to commence. Choosing MacDonald's Corps of the Army of Italy, he instructed them to destroy the Austrian center, which was south of Wagram. Using the formation of a hollow oblong and receiving support from the Imperial Guard artillery, MacDonald's troops managed to split the Austrian army successfully. Only 1,500 Austrians out of 8,000 survived this attack. Archduke Charles knew that the reinforcements promised by his brother, Archduke John, would not arrive in time. Therefore, he urged his army to begin a phased retreat around 2:30 p.m.

The French had won the battle, but at what cost? Napoleon and his allies lost around 32,000 soldiers in the bloody battle. While many died, others sustained severe wounds. They lost forty guns. The Austrians took 7,000 prisoners. It did not help that Napoleon utilized his skilled men and costly equipment for engaging in bloody frontal attacks. Around 23,000 Austrians either died or sustained wounds. Around 10,000 men went missing, but many returned to their respective units later. They lost 20 guns. Regardless of everything, the Austrians were able to retreat in good order. Napoleon's victory felt hollow, for it became clear to the world that if all came together as a combined force, they could beat Napoleon Bonaparte of France.

The Battle of Talavera, in July 1809, was, once again, a confrontation between the forces of Great Britain and that of France. King Joseph Bonaparte commanded 46,000 French soldiers. General Jourdan took up the role of advisor. The army had eighty guns. The combined forces of Great Britain and Spain numbered 52,000 soldiers. General Cuesta had control over 32,000 Spaniards. The overall command lay in the hands of Sir Arthur Wellesley. The battle took place at Talavera, a place located on the banks of the River Tagus. There were large, open plains next to the river, stretching all the way to the hills in the north. These plains turned into a battlefield for some days.

Sir Arthur Wellesley crossed into Spain via Portugal on July 2, 1809. He desired to attain the cooperation of the Spanish armies under the command of General Cuesta and General Venegas, for launching an attack on the French forces in Madrid. These forces had occupied Madrid too, without fear, since Joseph Bonaparte was the King of Spain. Emperor Napoleon had foisted a monarch of his choice upon the people of Spain, without consulting them. Wellesley was aware that the Spaniards were not too fond of their new king. To add insult to injury, Napoleon had also decided in 1809 that France must annex Holland, where he'd installed his brother as ruler. However, King Louis refused to obey his brother and abdicated instead of turning over the country, fleeing to various countries and occupying himself with literary pursuits. France took over Holland completely on July 9, 1810.

Now, Joseph Bonaparte had some aggressive plans up his sleeve too. He wanted to make use of Marshal Soult's troops to launch an invasion against Portugal. However, Wellesley had managed to make short work of Soult's troops earlier, making sure that they quit Portugal forever. Now, he wanted to attack Marshal Claude Victor and his corps near Talavera. General Cuesta expressed eagerness to fall in with Wellesley plans. Thus, the combined British-Spanish troops readied themselves for a battle on July 20. From July 22 onwards, the British began to keep a keen lookout for Victor and his forces. Marshal Soult gained early information about Wellesley's advance, learning that he had positioned his troops in the north. He instructed Claude Victor to hold off the combined forces of Britain and Spain for some time, until Soult was able to move to the south and place an army of 30,000 men between his base in Portugal and Wellesley's troops. Unfortunately, Victor could not manage the attacks against his troops for long. He withdrew, only to have Cuesta and his Spanish forces pursue the French forces.

When Cuesta reached Torrijos, a place that was 45 miles to the east, he came face to face with Joseph Bonaparte's army of 46,000 soldiers. Unable to defeat him, Cuesta and his forces beat a retreat. They joined Wellesley at Talavera. While pursuing the Spanish forces, the French Advance Guard encountered a brigade belonging to the British infantry. The brigade suffered heavy casualties during the skirmish that followed. By the evening of July 26, the combined forces of Britain and Spain deployed themselves at Talavera. They were aware that the Spanish-occupied Talavera would provide them with adequate support. Therefore, they settled down in an area to the north of the town and lay in wait for the French forces. The British occupied a line of high ground which stretched away towards the north. They remained behind the Spanish positions. The line ended at Cerro de Medellin. A narrow valley lay between the Cerro de Medellin and the mountains of the Sierra de Segurilla. However, Wellesley favored the high ground, for it proved apt for a defensive battle to take place.

Soon enough, Marshal Victor's Corps put in an appearance. His corps formed the French advance that had been pursuing the retreating Spanish troops, and surprised the British brigade. The French decided to launch an attack on the Cerro de Medellin on the evening of July 27, 1809. This feature highlighted the British line, and Victor wanted no delay in assaulting them. He did not care that it was nearing nighttime. General Ruffin's division initiated the attack against the British troops. In fact, the French troops had already climbed to the summit of the Cerro de Medellin, before the British even woke up to the fact that the French had arrived! As a result, there was immense confusion in the British ranks. However, the forces soon recovered. General Hill gathered a reserve brigade and drove Ruffin's troops away from the Cerro de Medellin. For the rest of the night, the

British troops stayed awake. They feared another sudden attack by the French forces.

On July 28, around 5:00 a.m., Marshal Claude Victor decided that Ruffin's men must return to the Cerro de Medellin. However, his troops would receive aid from a battery of fifty guns as they climbed the hill. However, the British were ready this time. Wellesley positioned his troops behind the crest of the hill. They lay down on the ground, to keep themselves out of sight. Furthermore, the crest protected them from the fire of the French artillery. When Ruffin's infantry reached the summit of the hill, the forces belonging to the British Twenty-Ninth and Forty-Eighth Foot stood up suddenly. They kept their bayonets at the ready and charged at the French forces. This way, they managed to push Ruffin's troops down the hill once again. In fact, they pursued them all the way to Portina Brook.

The British retaliation forced the French to rethink their strategies. The battle came to a halt for two hours as Joseph Bonaparte initiated a group discussion. The members of the group were Claude Victor, Jourdan (chief of staff) and Sebastiani. Marshal Victor insisted that Sebastiani take up the assault of the British right, just at the junction where the British troops linked up with the Spanish formations. This time around, he, and not Ruffin, would take his troops up the Cerro de Medellin once again. Joseph was so eager for a victory that he immediately acquiesced.

According to plan, Sebastiani's columns attacked the British right. This was the point where the hills were lowest. However, after a bitter battle, Sebastiani's troops had to retreat. The Seventh Fusiliers and the Fifty-Third Foot took care to see that they did not return. Then, Sebastiani's right column launched an assault on the British Foot Guards and the Eighty-Third Foot. This time, too, the French troops failed. The guards drove them back and even pursued them. However, a French battery came to the rescue. A fusillade of shots sufficed to create confusion amongst the British troops in this area. Sebastiani's men returned to the field, in order to attack the guards once more. Sensing that his troops were under fire, Wellesley brought up the Forty-Eighth Foot. The Guards were able to re-form behind this division. As a result, the British were able to repulse the dangerous counterattack launched by the French troops.

While all this was going on, Ruffin's division decided to launch a third attack on the Cerro de Medellin. Ruffin's men were not very enthusiastic, but had to follow orders. This time, too, they had no success. As for Claude Victor and his troops, they moved to the valley, which lay to the north of the

Cerro de Medellin. Victor's right-hand division strove to outflank the British line. Witnessing this, Wellesley instructed Anson's cavalry brigade to charge at Victor's infantry. However, this move backfired. The French were aware that there was a hidden defile. However, the cavalry did not know this. The First Light Dragoons associated with the King's German Legion, plunged into the defile. The Twenty-Third Light Dragoons, however, met with no mishap, and charged on. They confronted the French infantry in squares, thereby suffering heavy casualties.

Despite all their bravery, the French forces simply could not stand up to the combined might of the British and Spanish forces. Their assaults gradually petered out. Joseph Bonaparte and his army beat a retreat during the night. They left behind several guns, which proved useful for the British-Spanish forces. The French did not lose just 17 guns. Around 7,268 soldiers died, sustained wounds or became prisoners of war. The British suffered 5,363 casualties. The men died, suffered wounds or became prisoners of the French Army. The next day, Wellesley received news that Marshal Soult and a 30,000-strong army were near to cutting a route to Portugal. He left Talavera, in order to reach the Portuguese border as quickly as possible.

Austria had initiated a war of liberation, wanting to be free of French control. However, the Battle of Wagram destroyed all its hopes. Additionally, Prussia had not stood up to its promise of offering help at the right time. This defeat led to the great Treaty of Schonbrunn on October 14, 1809, signed at Schloss Schonbrunn in Vienna.

According to the treaty's terms, Austria had to give up around 32,000 square miles (83,000 square kilometers) of territory. Even the 3,500,000 inhabitants living in this area became France's "property"! France gained Trieste, Fiume, Istria, a major portion of Carniola, most of Carinthia and a part of Croatia. Russia received a reward for backing Napoleon, in the form of the Grand Duchy of Warsaw, the Tarnapol section of East Galcia, Lunlin and Krakow as parts of West Galicia. Bavaria received half of Hausruckviertel, Salzburg, the Innviertel and Berchtesgaden. This was not all. Napoleon demanded a huge indemnity from Austria too. It had to agree to break all trade and diplomatic relations with Great Britain. Finally, the nation had to reduce its military strength to about 150,000 soldiers. Because of the treaty, a truce existed between France and Austria for some time.

In 1811, Tsar Alexander withdrew his support for the Continental System. Since Spain, Portugal and Russia demonstrated sympathy and support for

Great Britain, Napoleon decided to launch aggressive measures against them. Believing that Russia needed a well-deserved lesson, he urged his army to march deep into Poland. His justification was that it was always better to take the war to the enemy camp and defeat them, no matter whatever it took. If going to Poland would make the Russians bend to his will, he was ready to march there! Napoleon's actions irked the British so much that they decided to launch a counter-blockade. Thus, the Continental System became one of the major causes for the eruption of the Anglo-American War in 1812.

The Death of Napoleon Bonaparte

Empress Josephine had failed to give the throne of France an heir. This had prompted Napoleon to wonder several times over the years if he should consider divorcing her. Then, when in late 1807, he left for Italy all alone, Josephine was miserable. She was always in tears and feared that the members of Napoleon's family were trying to poison her. This was because she often suffered from bouts of indigestion. Thus, when Napoleon decided to travel to Bavaria to battle with the Austrians in April 1809, Josephine forced him to take her with him. He made sure that she had comfortable lodgings in Strasbourg, while he went about his business. He also visited Countess Walewska at times. She was his favorite mistress and became pregnant with Napoleon's child. Her pregnancy was the deciding factor for Napoleon as he realized that he was not at fault for Josephine being childless. Towards the end of November 1809, he finally told Josephine that he wished to divorce her. She did not take the announcement lightly and threw temper tantrums. However, Napoleon went ahead with his plans.

After the announcement, the court annulled both the couple's religious and civil marriages. The official ceremonies took place in the throne room at the Palace of Tuileries on December 15, 1809.

Napoleon expressed his gratitude towards his wife for her tenderness and devotion but explained that he believed that it would be best for France if they separated. Josephine gave her consent to the divorce, with her hands shaking all the time. Then, the couple affixed their signatures to the record of the proceedings. Soon after, Josephine left for her chateau at Malmaison, carrying all her favorite possessions with her.

Despite his divorce, Napoleon made sure that Josephine was never short of money and that she continued to receive respect as the Empress Dowager. She died in 1814, at the age of fifty, possibly of a broken heart. Napoleon could only comment that she had truly loved him, had she not?

Napoleon expressed an interest in Grand Duchess Anna Pavlovna, the youngest sister of Tsar Alexander I. However, neither the tsar nor his mother agreed to the union. Then Napoleon offered to marry the twenty-seven-year-old Princess Maria Augusta of Saxony. However, this idea did not work either. Finally, he chose the eighteen-year-old Archduchess of Austria, Marie Louise. She was the daughter of Emperor Francis I, the head of the House of Habsburg. Obviously, Marie Louise was not too keen to marry a man who was twenty-two years older than she was and who had been her country's worst enemy until then. Marie-Antoinette had been Marie's great aunt. They had guillotined her during the French Revolution. However, when her father brought Napoleon's proposal to her, the obedient daughter bowed to his wishes.

Marshal Berthier affixed his signature to the marriage contract on March 9, 1810. So did the Austrian Foreign Minister, Clemens von Metternich. Marie Louise's dowry, comprised of 500,000 francs, reached Napoleon in the form of rolls of gold ducats. Thereafter, Marie Louise made a formal announcement about renouncing her right of succession to the Austrian throne. Marie Louise married the French Emperor by proxy on March 11, 1810. The wedding took place at the Augustinian Church, Vienna, wherein her uncle Charles took up the role of Napoleon Bonaparte.

The Beginning of the End

It is said that the once fearsome and twice-defeated Emperor Bonaparte was highly admired by Lord Byron. To the master English poet Byron, Napoleon was the best Romantic hero there could possibly be. For him, Bonaparte fit the image of a hated, hunted, shunned, flawed but brilliant mind. There are still people even today who admire Napoleon for his achievements. Thus, it is no wonder that the topic of his death is still hotly discussed and researched.

One of the most popular and widely accepted theories is that Bonaparte died at the hands of his captors. He was slowly fed poison by them, and he met the end of his life helplessly, without being able to do anything about it. This was such a popular and easy-to-accept theory that it was considered as the truth for a very long time until recent findings proved otherwise.

In the words of Dr. Robert Genta of Southwestern Medical Center of the University of Texas, Dallas: "Sorry to disappoint!" Genta stated that Napoleon's doctor got it right the first time. Napoleon had indeed died of pancreatic cancer which had reached an advanced, incurable stage.

In order to understand the circumstances which led to the death of Napoleon, it is important to understand his final days.

As per the Act of Abdication of Napoleon, the Allied powers had declared that Emperor Napoleon was the only reason why peace could not be restored in Europe. While all other countries were making compromises and joining forces, Napoleon stood firm on his choice of how France should be governed. Under pressure, Napoleon did not agree to change his ways but instead removed himself from the picture. Faithful to the oath that he had made, on April 11, 1814, he declared that he was renouncing the thrones of France and Italy. This declaration was not just limited himself but also extended to his heirs. He added that there was no personal sacrifice that he was not ready to make, even that of his life, as long as it was in the best interests of France.

As a part of his abdication, Napoleon was exiled to the island of Elba. Although Napoleon was the sovereign ruler of Elba and was allowed to retain the title of emperor, he was not happy. He decided to take his own life and consumed a pill that he had carried around with him, thinking that he would have to use it after being captured by the Germans. His first attempt at committing suicide was not successful, however. The pill had perhaps been weakened over the long period of time he'd had it. Thus, rather than dying, Bonaparte was forced to live a shunned life, alone, separated from his son and wife who had to flee to Austria and taken refuge.

While at Elba, Bonaparte did not give up all of his old ways. He worked vigorously to rouse the spirits of the natives there. Due to his efforts, the emperor-by-nature managed to create a batch of naval and army troops. He even saw to the development of the place by ordering and overseeing the creation of iron mines, roads and various other infrastructure projects. True to his nature, Bonaparte sought order and law in Elba, although he was an exiled ruler.

This meant that there was a radical change in the way the rules and law of the island country operated, and even in the educational system. Being a forward thinker and wanting to continue his good governance, Napoleon also ensured his people were using modern techniques of agriculture.

It seemed that things were going relatively well for the exiled emperor when Bonaparte received a very personal blow with the tragic news of the death of his former wife, Josephine. So deeply hurt and bereft was Bonaparte that he shut himself off from the rest of the world for two whole days to mourn her death. Although he had remarried, he had always insisted that Josephine retain her royal title and perhaps had always felt very bad that he had to divorce her and marry someone else for the sake of an heir.

A Revived Bonaparte

Perhaps prompted by the rumors that were floating around that he was to be exiled again, this time to an even more remote island in the Atlantic Ocean, Bonaparte managed to escape Elba with 700 men on the brig *Inconstant* on February 26, 1815. Little did Bonaparte know that all his efforts to bring back his old days of glory would never bear fruit. Just two days later, he reached the French mainland at Golfe-Juan and decided to proceed further north.

Alerted to his arrival and threatened by the power he could still wield, the powers that be sent the Fifth Regiment to capture Bonaparte and bring him in for a royal trial. The regiment did come into contact with the emperor but what happened next was quite astonishing. On March 7, 1815, when he faced the Fifth Regiment, Bonaparte dismounted from his horse and walked towards the soldiers, all alone. He stood there, right before them and within gunshot range, and yelled, "Here I am. Kill your emperor, if you wish." So moved was the regiment by the bravery and strength of Bonaparte that instead of killing him, they decided to follow his lead and shouted, "Vive L'Empereur!"

Ney, a member of the regiment, had promised the Bourbon king, Louis XVII, that he would not only capture Bonaparte, but would bring him before the king in Paris in an iron cage. Face to face with Napoleon, however, and impressed by his former emperor, he ended up kissing Napoleon's hands and decided to throw his weight behind him. Completely forgotten was his oath of allegiance to the king. The two men decided to combine their forces and head towards Paris, shoulder to shoulder.

Fearing the growing power of Napoleon, who now had a larger army under him, King Louis XVII fled Paris. A highly unpopular monarch, he lacked the political backing to face Napoleon. However, there were some who were not as cowardly as King Louis XVII and decided to take action. As a result of the joint efforts of various nations, a huge army of 150,000 men was created to tackle Bonaparte. The Congress of Vienna, which had declared Bonaparte an outlaw, was comprised of countries such as Prussia, Russia, Austria and Great Britain.

On March 20, Napoleon reached Paris and ruled it for a period now known as the Hundred Days. Things began to look even better from him at the beginning of June, when he had control of over 200,000 men in his army. Strengthened by a vast army, Napoleon decided to an attack those who were still out for his blood. He decided to break the ties with the British and Prussian armies, which had now decided to jointly attack him. Under the guidance of Napoleon, the French Army of the north breached the frontiers of the United Kingdom of Netherlands, now known as Belgium.

The Duke of Wellington and Gebhard Leberecht von Blucher jointly led the coalition armies which attacked Napoleon's troops. This attack will forever be remembered as the Battle of Waterloo. On June 18, 1815, while being heavily attacked by Wellington's army and later suffering because of the Prussian intrusion of the right flank, the French Army was forced to concede defeat. It was driven away from the field.

Napoleon returned to Paris to find the situation there, too, had worsened. After seeing him suffer a huge and humiliating defeat, Napoleon found that the lawmakers and citizens of Paris no longer wanted to submit to him as an emperor. After realizing that he would never be able to reign his beloved country again, Bonaparte abdicated the throne again on June 22, this time in favor of his son. Three days later, he removed himself from Paris and opted to settle down in Malmaison, the former palace of his true love, Josephine. While Napoleon was leaving Paris to travel to Malmaison, which lay on the western bank of Seine river about eleven miles west of Paris, the coalition forces returned to complete their job. They were on the hunt for Bonaparte, wanting to capture him and ensure that King Louis XVII was restored to his former royal position.

As soon as Bonaparte heard of his imminent arrest, he fled to Rochefort. At this stage, people wanted him captured, dead or alive. From Rochefort, Bonaparte intended to flee to the United States. By then, however, every exit port was being blocked by the British forces. On July 15, 1895, Napoleon was forced to request asylum from British Captain Frederick Maitland, who was commanding the HMS *Bellerophon*.

The Final Countdown

The British regime decided to accept Napoleon's request for asylum and exiled him once more, this time to the island of St. Helena. The rumors turned out to be true because this was indeed a very remote island in the Atlantic Ocean, roughly 1,870km west of the African coast. Napoleon was housed at Longwood House beginning December 1815. It was an extremely ramshackle, rundown house that was badly in need of repairs. In addition to the poor conditions of the house, the weather was not great. The house was located in a place that was almost permanently damp, windswept and overall very unhealthy.

The *Times* published an article that, indirectly, the British regime was trying its utmost to hasten Bonaparte's death by housing him in such utterly unhealthy conditions. Indeed, Napoleon voiced his complaints about the poor living conditions and his deteriorating health to his custodian, Hudson Lowe, and to the island's governor. Even those who were appointed to attend to Napoleon complained about the "catarrhs, colds, poor provisions and damp flooring." Modern-day studies have found that the copper arsenide that was used in the wallpaper of Longwood House was probably one of the factors that led to Napoleon's arsenic poisoning and death.

Bonaparte, with the help of the few people who were assigned to his care, started writing his memoirs, in which he liberally complained about his pathetic living conditions. Adding to the insult was a further cut in Bonaparte's expenses by Lowe, who also forbade any gifts being made to Napoleon by those who acknowledged him to be a royal king. All those who were appointed to take care of Napoleon were made to sign a legal agreement that tied them to the exiled prisoner for an indefinite period of time.

It was during this time that, despite his failing health, Napoleon managed to write about one of his favorite war kings and idols—Julius Caesar. Under the tutelage of Count Emmanuel de Las Cases, Napoleon spent most of his final days in Saint Helena improving upon his English by reading more and more English books and newspapers. One of the main reasons for his increased interest in English was the complete lack of access to French newspapers and books, as directed by the people who held him captive. Despite the many rumors that were circulated that Napoleon was trying to make another bid to escape the island, there was, in fact, no such attempt on his part. Perhaps he knew of his failing health conditions and also knew that he wouldn't be able to succeed in any further political attempts to regain his former state of glory.

Beginning in February 1821, Napoleon's health began worsening at a much more rapid rate. It was at this time that Napoleon decided to make amends with the divine and reconciled with the Catholic Church. Sadly, the mighty ruler didn't live for too long after that. Barely a few months later, on May 5, 1821, Napoleon passed away after he confessed and underwent the final Catholic rites of Extreme Unction and Viaticum in the presence of Father Ange Vignali. Napoleon's final words were: "France, l'armée, tête d'armée, Josephine," which can be translated as "France, the army, the head of the army, Josephine."

In honor of Napoleon's death, a death mask was created, although no one can confirm who created it. One of Napoleon's final wishes was that he be buried on Saint Helena, in the Valley of the Willows. Later, however, Louise Philippe I sought and obtained permission from the British to bring Napoleon's mortal remains back to his beloved France. On December 15, 1840, Louis Philippe I ensured a state funeral was held for Napoleon Bonaparte, once one of the most beloved and looked-upon emperors of France. The hearse's royal procession began from l'Arc de Triomphe, proceeded to the Champs-Elysees, the Place de la Concorde, the Esplanade des Invalides and, finally, ended at the St. Jerome Chapel. Napoleon's remains were left in the cupola of the chapel until his tomb could be completed by Louis Visconti. Once the tomb was ready, Napoleon's remains were transferred into a porphyry stone sarcophagus that was placed in a crypt under the dome at Les Invalides.

One of Napoleon's physicians, and the doctor who led the team which performed the autopsy of the dead emperor, Francois Carlo Antommarchi, initially stated the death was caused by stomach cancer. Antommarchi, however, did not sign the official report. Most people remained unaware of the real reason for Napoleon's death, as a result. Antommarchi had also found traces of a stomach ulcer, which the British publicized in order to escape criticism from people all over the world on the way Napoleon had been housed in his final days.

Louis Marchand, one of the valets who was devoted to Napoleon and who was with him during his final days, was fond of writing and maintained a memoir. His diaries were published in 1955. As a result of his diaries, new theories about the death of Napoleon were put forward. In 1961, Sten Forshufvud published a report in the scientific journal *Nature* which included some of Marchand's theories. During Napoleon's lifetime, one of the most popular methods employed by people to get rid of people quietly, without arousing any suspicion, was arsenic poisoning. It was such a popular option because it is very difficult to detect any traces of arsenic, especially when it is administered in very small doses over a long period of time. Sten Forshufvud and his co-author Ben Weider noted that Napoleon's body was found to be in remarkably good condition when it was dug up after several years and moved back to France in 1840. Arsenic helps keep a body from decomposing at its usual rate. Apart from being a lethal preservative, arsenic is also known to cause a person to feel constantly thirsty. In his final days, Napoleon was almost always thirsty and drank huge quantities of orgeat syrup, a liquid that contained a high amount of cyanide due to the almonds that were used to add to its flavor.

The authors stated that as a part of his treatment, potassium tartrate was used liberally, which meant that Napoleon's stomach could not fully flush out the toxic components, thus making him very thirsty all the time. They further noted that the calomel that was administered to Napoleon could have been given in excessive quantities, causing extensive tissue damage. Toxicologist Patrick Kintz was one person who supported the murder theory.

There have been several studies over the years that have lent credence to the murder theory. In 2008, there was a report published based on the study of Napoleon's hair belonging to different years of his life as compared with hair from other people during that period, including his family and contemporaries. It was found that the level of arsenic in Napoleon's hair was much higher than was safe, but other people's hair also had extremely high levels. In fact, arsenic was very popularly used in different ways back then, and Napoleon may already have been exposed to a toxic amount of arsenic during his younger days, primarily because of the arsenic-laced dyes and glues used in those days. The exposure was so high that the hair samples collected from people alive in those days had 100-time higher arsenic levels than the modern-day average!

The final conclusion of all the studies was that although arsenic was a major contributor to the death of Napoleon, it was not administered by people who wanted him dead. The presence of arsenic in Napoleon's body was primarily due to his lifelong living conditions and exposure to everyday things that contained the lethal compound. Therefore, the final verdict was that Napoleon's death was caused due to a combination of a peptic ulcer and gastric cancer.

Several reputed scientists, including Genta, have confirmed that even if someone had attempted to treat Napoleon by removing him from St. Helena, it would have been an impossible task because he had a very advanced cancer and wouldn't have been able to withstand the move from one place to another.

www.ingramcontent.com/pod-product-compliance
Lightning Source LLC
Chambersburg PA
CBHW071231070526
44583CB00017B/2128